205

Questions Children Ask about God, Heaven and Angels

205

Questions Children Ask about God, Heaven and Angels

with answers from the Bible
for busy parents

Written by
David R. Veerman, M.Div.
James C. Galvin, Ed.D.
James C. Wilhoit, Ph.D.
Bruce B. Barton, D.Min.
Daryl J. Lucas
Richard Osborne

Illustrated by Lillian Crump

Testament Books
New York

This 2003 edition is published by Testament Books, an imprint of Random House Value Publishing, a division of Random House Inc., New York, by arrangement with Tyndale House Publishers, Inc.

Random House
New York • Toronto • London • Sydney • Auckland
www.randomhouse.com

Printed in the United States of America

A catalog record for this title is available from the Library of Congress.

ISBN: 0-517-22246-9

9 8 7 6 5 4 3 2 1

CONTENTS

Part I

Questions Children Ask about God

Written by
David R. Veerman, M.Div.
James C. Galvin, Ed.D.
James C. Wilhoit, Ph.D.
Daryl J. Lucas
Richard Osborne

CONTENTS

THE BIBLE

THE CHURCH

INTRODUCTION

Children are filled with questions as they begin to discover the world and learn how to ask. Some of their questions are simple and easy to answer, like, "Do I have to eat these peas?" and "Can I stay up?" But many of their queries are complex and seem impossible to answer, especially when children ask why. And when they move into the spiritual realm, the questions can be downright profound.

Of course, an easy response to anything children ask (a response that is used, unfortunately, by many parents) is, "Just because!" or "Because I said so!" That may be a response, but it's not an answer, and it is certainly unsatisfying to the child.

Instead, parents should handle their children's questions with loving care, seeing them for what they are—bubbles of curiosity, fresh moments of honesty, and exciting opportunities to teach.

That's why this book was written, to give parents help in answering their children's questions about God, the Bible, life after death, Jesus, and other spiritual issues.

The questions in this book are real; that is, they were really asked by boys and girls. Out of scores of questions, 101 were chosen to answer. And speaking of answers, each one has been carefully thought through and crafted, not as the last, exhaustive word on the subject, but as an honest answer for young, inquiring minds.

Related questions, key verses, and other Bible references are also included with each question.

As you answer your child's questions, remember to . . .

- Look for the question behind the question. For example, when a little boy asks, "Does the devil have claws?" (question 73), he probably wants to know, "Can the devil hurt me?"
- Be careful about making up an answer when you don't have one and when the Bible is silent (for example, "What does my angel do?"—question 71). Too often, children will later lump faith with other stories and superstitions they've been taught and then discovered were false. Be honest with your answers. If you don't have one, say so. Or suggest that you look for the answer together.
- Be ready for follow-up questions. Your answer may lead to more questions. That's the mark of a good answer—it makes the child think.
- Make your answers concrete. Children think in very literal and concrete terms, so abstract concepts such as "heaven," "justification," and "God's will" are difficult for them to understand until their ability to think abstractly naturally develops. But children can learn to pray, obey what God wants, and read and memorize the Bible.
- Always take children's questions seriously, even when they sound funny to you. It's amazing what little eyes see and little ears hear. One little girl ended a prayer with, "In Jesus' name, M&M." Another one asked about "the turtle's life" after hearing her father talk about "eternal life."

Jesus said, "Let the little children come to me. Don't stop them. For the Kingdom of Heaven belongs to such as these" (Matthew 19:14). We can unintentionally hinder children by ignoring their questions, not taking the time to answer them, or not taking them seriously. We can also hinder children by our own example, living as if faith in Christ does not make a difference.

May God help us as we tenderly care for these precious lives he has entrusted to us.

CREATION

Q: WHY DID GOD CREATE THE WORLD?

JASON'S IMAGINATION

A: God created the world and everything in it because he enjoys making things, and he wanted to be with us. God created people because he wanted to have friends, men and women, boys and girls, with whom he could share his love. He created the world for them to live in and enjoy.

KEY VERSES: *In the beginning God created the heavens and the earth. . . . Then God looked over all that he had made. It was excellent in every way. (Genesis 1:1, 31)*

RELATED VERSES: *Genesis 1:1–2:1; Psalm 19:1; Isaiah 45:7*

RELATED QUESTIONS: *Why did God rest when all he did was speak? Why did God create water when there was milk?*

NOTE TO PARENTS: *This question is a good opportunity to tell your children that God's plan involves them. God created the world and everything in it—including your children—so that he could have people to love.*

Q: ## HOW DID GOD CREATE THE EARTH?

A: Whenever we make something, like a craft, a drawing, or a sand castle, we have to start with special materials, like clay, string, glue, paper, crayons, and sand. We can't even imagine creating something out of nothing—by just saying the words and making it appear. But God is so powerful that he can do what is impossible for us. That includes making anything he wants, even creating things from nothing. That's what it means to be God—he can do anything.

KEY VERSES: *Before anything else existed, there was God's Son. He was the Word, and he was with God. He has always been alive and is himself God. He created everything there is. Nothing exists that he didn't make. (John 1:1-3)*

RELATED VERSES: *Genesis 1:1-2; Hebrews 1:10; 2 Peter 3:5-6*

RELATED QUESTIONS: *Why did it take God six days to create the world? What was everything like before God created the world?*

Q: WERE THERE DINOSAURS ON THE ARK?

A: Dinosaurs are popular today. They're on television and in the comics. We even have dinosaur stuffed toys. Scientists say that these unusual animals lived and became extinct over a hundred million years ago, so it's natural to wonder where they fit into the Bible. Most Bible experts believe that dinosaurs died out many years before the great flood that we read about in Genesis. So there wouldn't have been any dinosaurs around to put on the ark. Another reason we don't read about dinosaurs in the Bible is that the Bible wasn't written to tell us everything. It's not a science textbook. The Bible tells us about people and God's plan for our life.

KEY VERSES: *[God is speaking] "Look at Behemoth, which I made just as I made you; it eats grass like an ox. Its strength is in its loins, and its power in the muscles of its belly. It makes its tail stiff like a cedar; the sinews of its thighs are knit together. Its bones are tubes of bronze, its limbs like bars of iron." (Job 40:15-19, NRSV)*

RELATED VERSES: *Genesis 7:1-24; John 1:3*

RELATED QUESTIONS: *Why don't we have dinosaurs today? Why aren't dinosaurs mentioned in the Bible? Where do dinosaurs fit into the Bible? Were there dinosaurs around with Adam and Eve?*

NOTE TO PARENTS: *The Bible doesn't mention dinosaurs, but it does say that God created everything (John 1:3). Some verses, like the one about Behemoth, talk about animals almost as big as dinosaurs.*

Q: WHY DID GOD MAKE MOSQUITOES?

A: When we're being attacked by mosquitoes, it's easy to wonder why God made pests and other animals that can harm us. When God created the world, it was perfect. Only after sin entered the picture did animals and human beings become enemies, causing humans to protect and defend themselves. So now mosquitoes try to feed off of us. They, in turn, become food for birds and bats. In the future, in the new heaven and new earth, animals won't hurt people or each other.

KEY VERSES: *In that day the wolf and the lamb will lie down together. And the leopard and goats will be at peace. Calves and fat cattle will be safe among lions. And a little child shall lead them all. The cows will graze among bears. Cubs and calves will lie down side by side. And lions will eat grass like the cows. Babies will crawl safely among deadly snakes. And a little child who puts his hand into a nest of adders will not be hurt. Nothing will hurt or destroy in all my holy mountain. And as the waters fill the sea, the earth will be full of the knowledge of the Lord. (Isaiah 11:6-9)*

RELATED VERSES: *Genesis 3:17-19; Romans 8:19-22*

RELATED QUESTIONS: *Why did God make bugs that bother us? Why did God make animals that we can't eat?*

People Fish & Chips

A: Sharks attack people because they are meat-eaters. When they are hungry, they will attack anything that looks good to eat. Sharks don't go looking for people to attack—they just react to what comes near them. The best thing to do is to be smart and stay away from sharks. When we go where we shouldn't go, we get into trouble—like walking in poison ivy or playing in a thunderstorm. There are dangers in the world, and we should be careful to avoid them.

KEY VERSES: *For wisdom will enter your heart, and knowledge will be pleasant to your soul. Discretion will protect you, and understanding will guard you. (Proverbs 2:10-11, NIV)*

RELATED VERSES: *Genesis 3:17-19; Numbers 21:6; Deuteronomy 32:24; Jeremiah 8:17; Ezekiel 34:25; Matthew 10:16*

RELATED QUESTIONS: *Why did God make animals that harm us? Why did God create poison ivy and poisonous plants?*

NOTE TO PARENTS: *The question of why God made animals that can harm us is answered earlier in Question 4. The answer according to Scripture is that we live in a sinful world (Genesis 3:14-19).*

A: God created spiders just as he made all the other animals. But there's a great difference between animals and human beings. People are created in God's image and are supposed to take care of all creation—including all animals and plants. God put people in charge of creation, but this does not mean we can harm and kill for fun or destroy the world as we please. We can kill animals and plants for food and to control their population; we can remove or kill spiders, insects, and so forth that threaten us or make it difficult for us to live. But we should be kind to animals when possible and take good care of the world.

KEY VERSE: *And God blessed them and told them, "Multiply and fill the earth and subdue it. You are masters of the fish and birds and all the animals." (Genesis 1:28)*

RELATED VERSES: *Genesis 1:20-25; Proverbs 12:10; Acts 10:9-16*

NOTE TO PARENTS: *Some children want to hurt animals, while others want to be compassionate. God's desire is for us to be compassionate and wise rulers of all animal life (Proverbs 12:10). This should not be taken to such an extreme that we think eating meat is wrong. God has provided animals as a source of food and has given us permission to eat meat (see Acts 10).*

Q: WHY DID GOD MAKE PEOPLE RED AND YELLOW, BLACK AND WHITE?

7

A: Can you imagine a world in which everyone looked the same—the same height, weight, color of hair, length of nose, color of eyes, size of ears, and color of skin? That would be boring—and how would we tell people apart? Instead, God created all kinds and colors of people. Some are tall; some are short; some are brown; some are pink; some have straight black hair; some have curly red hair. They are all special to God. Don't you just love the differences and what makes you special? God does!

KEY VERSE: *In this new life your nation or race or education or social group means nothing. Christ is what matters, and he has been given to all. (Colossians 3:11)*

RELATED VERSES: *Jeremiah 13:23; Acts 17:26*

RELATED QUESTION: *How did people get different color skin when Adam and Eve were only one color?*

8

A: Although people may talk about creatures in outer space, no one really knows whether there is life on other planets. Most of the talk about other life forms comes from make-believe movies and what people imagine *might* be true. But if there is life in other parts of the universe, God is in charge of it because God is in charge of the whole universe. God created *everything,* and he is the God of all life everywhere, no matter where it may be.

KEY VERSE: *Christ created everything in Heaven and earth. He created the things we can see and the things we can't see. All kings and kingdoms, rulers and powers were made by Christ. He made them for his own use and glory. (Colossians 1:16)*

RELATED VERSES: *Genesis 1:1; 1 Chronicles 29:11-12*

RELATED QUESTIONS: *Are there aliens in outer space? Why did God make Mars and Jupiter?*

Q: HOW DOES GOD MAKE THE SUN AND MOON GO UP AND DOWN?

9

A: God made powerful laws to govern the universe. These laws control the movements of the sun, moon, earth, and other planets and stars. For example, one law called "gravity" draws objects toward each other. Other natural laws control the weather. Many forces determine whether the day will be sunny or cloudy, warm or cold, such as the heat from the sun, the currents in the ocean, the wind, and many others. God set up the rules that make all these forces work together. And because God controls the entire universe, he can interrupt the laws if he wants to—bring rain to dry land or bright sunshine to flooded areas. How powerful God must be to control all that!

KEY VERSE: *The heavens are telling the glory of God. They are a great display of what God can do. (Psalm 19:1)*

RELATED VERSES: *Joshua 10:13; 1 Kings 18:1ff.; 2 Kings 20:8-11; 2 Chronicles 7:12ff.; Psalm 19:1-6; 104:19; 148:3; Hebrews 1:2-3*

RELATED QUESTIONS: *How does God make the weather? Can God make the weather so that it'll be sunny tomorrow?*

NOTE TO PARENTS: *Part of this is a science issue. If your children are wondering how the forces of nature work, don't be afraid of encouraging them to learn more about the natural sciences. The power and wonder of nature can be used to inspire awe and worship of God. The heavens declare his glory! (See Psalm 19.)*

ADAM

AND

EVE

Q: WHY DID GOD MAKE PEOPLE?

10

A: People are special creations, not just different animals. God created people to be his friends and to take care of the world. Unlike animals, human beings can talk to each other and to God. People are the only part of God's marvelous creation that can be friends with God. And he created them perfect—that's why Adam and Eve were not ashamed of their nakedness. But people are also the only ones who can sin.

KEY VERSES: *Then God said, "Let us make a man—someone like ourselves. He will be the master of all life upon the earth and in the skies and in the seas." So God made man like his Maker. Like God did God make man. Man and maid did he make them. (Genesis 1:26-27)*

RELATED VERSES: *Genesis 2:4-7; Psalm 8:4-5; 139:13-18*

RELATED QUESTIONS: *Why did God make people in addition to animals? Why did God make women?*

11

A: God made Adam and Eve, the first human beings, by using material that he had already made. God formed Adam just the way he wanted him to look and then brought Adam to life. God made Eve from part of Adam so that she would match him perfectly.

KEY VERSES: *The time came when the Lord God formed a man's body. He made it from the dust of the ground. Then he breathed into it the breath of life. And man became a living person. . . . Then the Lord God caused the man to fall into a deep sleep. He took one of the man's ribs. Then he closed up the place from which he had taken it. Then he made the rib into a woman, and brought her to the man. (Genesis 2:7, 21-22)*

RELATED VERSES: *Genesis 1:26–2:25; 3:19; 1 Timothy 2:13*

RELATED QUESTIONS: *Why did God make Eve from Adam's rib? Why did God make us out of dust?*

NOTE TO PARENTS: *A young child's concrete understanding can be a barrier to understanding this because the creation of Adam and Eve was a miracle. Explaining it as such may be the best approach, especially if your child is asking about the exact process that God used.*

Q: WHAT DID ADAM AND EVE "DRESS" THE LAND WITH?

12

A: The word *dress* that is used in some Bible versions means "take care of" or "tend." So when God told Adam and Eve to "dress" the land, he was telling them to take care of the rest of his creation.

KEY VERSE: *And the Lord God took the man, and put him into the garden of Eden to dress it and to keep it. (Genesis 2:15, KJV)*

RELATED VERSES: *Genesis 18:7; Deuteronomy 28:39; 2 Samuel 12:4*

NOTE TO PARENTS: *This kind of question is a good example of why it is important to choose an age-appropriate translation of the Bible for your child. There are many excellent translations from which to choose. The best one for your child is the one that uses words that he or she already knows.*

13

A: When God created animals and plants, he gave them the ability to reproduce themselves. The same is true with Adam and Eve—God created them with the ability to make babies. Adam and Eve had babies; then, when those children grew up, they got married and also had children. Those children also grew up and had babies. As time went on, there were more and more people on the earth. And although God didn't make each person the same way he created Adam and Eve, he was still involved with the creation of each one, watching over and putting him or her (and you) together just right.

KEY VERSE: *Then Adam lay with Eve his wife. She conceived and gave birth to a son, Cain (meaning "I have created"). For, as she said, "With God's help, I have created a man!" Her next child was his brother, Abel. Abel became a shepherd. Cain was a farmer. (Genesis 4:1-2)*

RELATED VERSES: *Genesis 1:28; 5:1-18; 6:1; Psalm 139: 13-18; Ezekiel 36:11; Hebrews 6:14*

RELATED QUESTIONS: *Did God make me the same way he made Adam? Did Eve have a belly button?*

NOTE TO PARENTS: *Many parents avoid this issue because they are uncomfortable talking about sex. Don't communicate nonverbally that this is a dirty or embarrassing topic. But at the same time, don't give children more information than they want or need.*

14

A: God gave Adam the job of naming the animals, much like when your parents might ask you to name your pet. Adam named the animals whatever he wanted. But Adam didn't speak English, so the names he used are not the ones we use today. Adam lived a very long time ago, and today each language has its own words for the animals in our world.

KEY VERSES: *So the Lord God formed from the soil every kind of animal and bird. He brought them to the man to see what he would call them. Whatever the man called them, that was their name. (Genesis 2:19-20)*

RELATED VERSES: *Acts 13:2; Colossians 4:17*

Q: WHY DID ADAM AND EVE EAT THE FORBIDDEN FRUIT IF GOD SAID NOT TO?

15

A: Adam and Eve were sinless and perfect when God created them. But they still could choose to do what was wrong (just like you can choose to do what you aren't supposed to). When the devil tempted them to eat the forbidden fruit, they chose to do it. Although people talk about Adam and Eve eating an "apple" in the Garden of Eden, we don't know what the fruit looked like or how it tasted. All we know is that it was the one fruit in that big, beautiful garden that they weren't supposed to eat. Adam and Eve ate the fruit because the devil started them thinking about what it would be like. Then he lied about God's rule to make them think that God was keeping something good from them. Pretty soon they wanted to eat the fruit more than they wanted to obey God's rule.

KEY VERSES: *The serpent was the craftiest of all the creatures the Lord God had made. So the serpent came to the woman. "Really?" he asked. "None of the fruit in the garden? God says you mustn't eat any of it?" "Of course we may eat it," the woman told him. "It's only the fruit from the tree at the center of the garden that we must not eat. God says we must not eat it or even touch it. If we do, we will die." "That's a lie" the serpent hissed. "You'll not die! God knows very well that as soon as you eat it you will become like him. Your eyes will be opened. You will be able to know good from evil!" The woman was convinced. How lovely and fresh-looking it was! And it would make her so wise! So she ate some of the fruit and gave some to her husband. He ate it too. (Genesis 3:1-6)*

RELATED VERSES: *Matthew 6:13; 26:41*

ADAM AND EVE

Q: WHY DIDN'T ADAM DIE WHEN GOD SAID HE WOULD?

16

A: When Adam and Eve disobeyed God and ate the fruit, sin entered the world. That was the first sin ever! And when sin came into the world, death came with it. There are two kinds of death, and both came to Adam and Eve and to the world. First, there is physical death. Although Adam and Eve didn't die immediately when they took a bite of the fruit, eventually they *would* die. From that moment on, all plants, animals, and humans would die eventually. Second, there is spiritual death. That means being separated from God, being his enemies instead of his friends. This death came to Adam and Eve, and to all of us, the moment they disobeyed God. The only way to avoid this death forever is to trust in Christ. That's why Jesus came to earth—to die in our place, for our sin, so that we might have eternal life!

KEY VERSES: *When Adam sinned, sin entered the whole human race. His sin spread death through all the world. Everything began to grow old and die because all sinned. . . . For this one man, Adam, brought death to many through his sin. But this one man, Jesus Christ, brought forgiveness to many through God's mercy. Adam's one sin brought the penalty of death to many. But Christ freely takes away many sins and gives new life instead. (Romans 5:12, 15-16)*

RELATED VERSES: *Hebrews 9:27; James 4:14*

17

A: God knows everything, even before it happens, so he knew that Adam and Eve were going to sin. Still, God was very disappointed with what Adam and Eve did. But because God loved them (and because he loves us), he made a way for the sin to be forgiven. God's plan was to send Jesus to die on the cross for Adam's, Eve's, and our sins. By trusting in Christ, we can have eternal life.

KEY VERSES: *Long ago, before he made the world, God chose us to be his very own. He did this because of what Christ would do for us. He decided then to make us holy in his eyes, without a single fault. We stand before him covered with his love. His plan has always been to adopt us into his own family. He would do this by sending Jesus Christ to die for us. And he did this because he wanted to! (Ephesians 1:4-5)*

RELATED VERSES: *John 2:23-25; Acts 17:26-27*

NOTE TO PARENTS: *The knowledge that God knows everything can give your children a sense of security. Children can't do anything that will surprise God. He may be happy or disappointed, but he won't be surprised. Also, be aware that your children may not understand what the word penalty means. So be prepared to offer a simple explanation.*

Q: WHAT DOES GOD LOOK LIKE?

18

A: No one knows what God "looks like" because God is invisible and doesn't have a physical body as we do. But we can learn about God and see what God acts like by learning about his Son, Jesus. In the Bible we can read about how Jesus lived, how he treated people, and what he taught. That's what God is like.

KEY VERSE: *Jesus replied, "Don't you even yet know who I am, Philip? And I have been with you for all this time! Anyone who has seen me has seen the Father! So why are you asking to see him?" (John 14:9)*

RELATED VERSES: *John 1:18; 5:37; 6:46; 1 John 3:2*

RELATED QUESTIONS: *Does God have a beard? Is God bald?*

Q: DOES GOD HAVE FRIENDS OR IS HE ALONE?

19

A: God doesn't have other "gods" to be friends with. He is the only God there is. God doesn't need friends the way we do; he is perfectly happy being alone. But God also wants to have friendship with us. In fact, God wants to be our closest friend. So he has done a lot to make friends with us and to have our friendship. That's why he created us, sent Jesus to save us, gave us the Bible, and gave us the church.

KEY VERSES: *And you are my friends if you obey me. I no longer call you slaves. For a master doesn't confide in his slaves. Now you are my friends. This is proved by the fact that I have told you all that the Father told me. (John 15:14-15)*

RELATED VERSES: *Genesis 1:26; John 17:3*

RELATED QUESTIONS: *Are there other gods? Does God ever get lonely?*

Q: WHERE DOES GOD LIVE?

20

A: Sometimes we think of God as though he were another person like us. And just as we can only be one place at a time and we need a place to live, we think that God is the same way. But God isn't limited to a physical body or to one place at a time. In fact, God lives everywhere, especially inside people who love him. We call church "God's house" because that's where people who love God gather together to worship him. But no matter where we are, God is with us. We can never be lost to his love. God also lives in heaven— eventually, we will live there, too.

KEY VERSES: *[Solomon is speaking] "But is it possible that God would live on earth? Why, even the skies and the highest heavens cannot hold you! This Temple I have built will not be able to hold you either! And yet, O Lord my God, you have heard and answered what I asked. Please watch over this Temple night and day. For this is the place you have promised to live. Please listen to my prayers here, whether by night or by day. Listen to every prayer of the people of Israel. Listen to them when they face this place to pray. Yes, hear in heaven where you live. And when you hear, forgive." (1 Kings 8:27-30)*

RELATED VERSES: *Psalm 139:7-12; Acts 17:24-29; Romans 8:38-39; Ephesians 4:8-10*

RELATED QUESTIONS: *Does God live in the mountains? Where is heaven? How can God live in my heart? Does God live in church? How can God be everywhere? Is God a person or a ghost? How big is God?*

Q: DOES GOD SLEEP, OR DOES HE JUST REST?

21

A: God does not have a physical body like us, so he doesn't need to sleep or eat. When the Bible says God "rests," it means he has stopped doing something. To us, that is like rest. But God doesn't get tired or worn out, so he doesn't need to rest the way we do. And when we go to sleep at night, God doesn't close his eyes too—he continues to watch over us.

KEY VERSES: *He will never let me stumble, slip, or fall. For he is always watching, never sleeping. (Psalm 121:3-4)*

RELATED VERSES: *Genesis 2:2; 1 Kings 18:27; Ecclesiastes 8:16-17*

RELATED QUESTIONS: *Will I be safe at night? What does God do in heaven? Does God eat?*

NOTE TO PARENTS: *This kind of question arises from the faulty thinking that God is just like people. Most false gods that have been made up by various cultures, such as those the Canaanites worshiped or the Greek gods, were much like comic book superheros—just like people with superhuman abilities. But God isn't just a greater human. Clearing up this question will correct this faulty way of thinking about God.*

Q: WHO CREATED GOD?

22

A: No one created God—he has always existed. We can't understand this because everything that we know has a beginning or an end. Each day has a morning and night; basketball games have an opening tip-off and a final buzzer; people are born and they die. But God has no beginning or end. He always was and always will be.

KEY VERSES: *Lord, through all the generations you have been our home! You were there before the mountains were made. You were there before the earth was formed. You are God without beginning or end. (Psalm 90:1-2)*

RELATED VERSES: *Hebrews 13:8; Revelation 1:8, 18*

RELATED QUESTIONS: *Where did God come from? Will God ever die? How old is God?*

Q: WHY CAN'T WE SEE GOD?

23

A: We can't see God because he's invisible. But we *can* see what he does. Balloons are filled with air that we can't see, but we see the balloon get big as the air is put in. Radio waves are invisible, but they exist. Just because we can't see God doesn't mean he isn't real. Believing that God is there even though we can't see him is *faith*. Someday, in heaven, we will see God face to face.

KEY VERSE: *We can see and understand only a little about God now. It is like we were looking at his reflection in a poor mirror. Someday we are going to see him face to face. Now all that I know is hazy and blurred. But then I will see everything clearly. I will see as clearly as God sees into my heart right now. (1 Corinthians 13:12)*

RELATED VERSES: *John 1:18; Colossians 1:15; 1 Timothy 1:17; Hebrews 11:27*

RELATED QUESTION: *Why doesn't God let everyone see him so everyone will believe him?*

NOTE TO PARENTS: *Young children struggle with this because of their concrete way of thinking. Using illustrations like the ones here are helpful, but still imperfect; we can't see air because it's molecules don't form a solid enough image for us to see, not because it has no physical form. In contrast, God is invisible to us because he is a spirit.*

Q: CAN CHRISTIANS HEAR GOD TALKING TO THEM?

24

A: In the Bible we read about people hearing God's voice. Today, the main way that God speaks to us is through the Bible. That's why it's called "God's Word"—the Bible is God's message to us. God may also speak to us through people and circumstances and in other ways. But God will never tell us to do something that goes against what he says in the Bible. And don't forget, God is with us all the time.

KEY VERSES: *Long ago God spoke in many different ways to our fathers. He spoke through the prophets in visions, dreams, and even face to face. Little by little he told them about his plans. But now in these days he has spoken to us through his Son. He has given his Son everything. Through his Son he made the world and everything there is. (Hebrews 1:1-2)*

RELATED VERSES: *1 Samuel 3:1-18; Psalm 119:1-24*

RELATED QUESTIONS: *How can I hear God? Does my heart have ears?*

Q: DAD, WHY DO I NEED TWO FATHERS, YOU AND GOD?

25

A: We call God "our Father" because he created us, watches over us, and provides everything we need. He's like a human father, only perfect. God has given us human fathers and mothers to take care of us on earth. That's why God tells children to obey their parents and their heavenly Father—it's for their own good.

KEY VERSE: *[Jesus is speaking] "You sinful men even know how to give good gifts to your children. So won't your Father in Heaven be sure to give good gifts to those who ask him for them?" (Matthew 7:11)*

RELATED VERSES: *Exodus 20:12; Ephesians 6:1-3*

RELATED QUESTIONS: *What does it mean that God is our Father? What's the same and different about human fathers and God? Why does God say kids have to obey their parents?*

Q: DOES GOD SEE EVERYTHING THAT WE DO?

26

A: Yes, God sees everything we do, both good and bad. We can't hide from him. God is happy when we do what is right and sad when we do wrong. God can reward us for doing what's right, even when no one else knows about it.

KEY VERSES: *[Elihu is speaking] "For God watches the deeds of all mankind. He sees them all. No darkness is thick enough to hide evil men from his eyes." (Job 34:21-22)*

RELATED VERSES: *Job 11:11; 31:4; Psalm 147:5; Matthew 10:28-31*

RELATED QUESTIONS: *Does God see the bad things I do? How can God know everything? How can God see everywhere?*

NOTE TO PARENTS: *This question may arise from a guilty conscience. Your child may want to talk about something that he or she did.*

JESUS

Q: IS JESUS GOD?

theolojikal answers Jason

27

A: Jesus is fully God. When he came to earth and was born of the Virgin Mary, Jesus also became a human being, a person like you. So Jesus is both God and man. As God, Jesus has always existed—he was not created when he was born. Instead, he willingly chose to take on a human body.

KEY VERSES: *Before anything else existed, there was God's Son. He was the Word, and he was with God. He has always been alive and is himself God. (John 1:1-2)*

RELATED VERSES: *John 1:14; 14:9; Colossians 1:15-18*

RELATED QUESTION: *Did God create Jesus?*

Q: HOW CAN GOD BE THREE PERSONS AND ONE PERSON AT THE SAME TIME?

28

A: We don't know *how* God can be three persons at the same time, but we know he is because the Bible tells us so. The idea of three in one (the Trinity) is very hard to understand. Some people use the example of water. Water can be a liquid, a gas, or a solid. We usually see water in liquid form, as when we use it for drinking or for taking a bath. But water can also be a gas, as when it turns to steam. And it can be a solid, in the form of ice. But whether liquid, gas, or solid, it's still water. In some ways God is like a family with father, mother, and child—three persons and one family. Just remember that the Trinity does not mean that we have three gods. There is one God with three persons. The Trinity also does not mean that God wears three hats, or takes on three roles, at different times. All three persons—Father, Son, and Holy Spirit—have always existed.

KEY VERSE: *[Jesus is speaking] "So now go and make disciples in all the nations. Baptize them into the name of the Father, the Son, and the Holy Spirit." (Matthew 28:19)*

RELATED VERSES: *Matthew 3:16-17; John 14:7, 9-10*

RELATED QUESTION: *Why are there three people in the Trinity?*

29

A: As a man, Jesus cried real tears when he was sad. God does not shed tears today, but he feels sad when people are hurting, when they disobey him, and when they don't believe in him. We can bring God joy by living as we should, showing love to others, and telling people about Christ.

KEY VERSE: *Tears came to Jesus' eyes. (John 11:35)*

RELATED VERSES: *Luke 19:41; John 11:33; Ephesians 4:30; Revelation 7:17*

RELATED QUESTION: *Does God have a heart?*

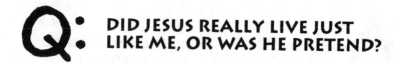

Q: DID JESUS REALLY LIVE JUST LIKE ME, OR WAS HE PRETEND?

30

A: Jesus is real. He came to earth and was born as a baby (we celebrate Jesus' birth at Christmas). And he lived like other ordinary people. Some stories we read and hear are made up and weren't meant to be taken as true. But the stories in the Bible really happened, and that's where we can read about Jesus.

KEY VERSE: *Christ was alive when the world began. I have seen him with my own eyes and listened to him speak. I have touched him with my own hands. He is God's message of life. (1 John 1:1)*

RELATED VERSES: *John 20:27; 1 Timothy 3:16; Hebrews 4:15*

Q: DID JESUS EVER DO ANYTHING BAD WHEN HE WAS LITTLE?

31

A: Jesus was born as a baby and grew up as a little boy and into a young man. When he was a child, Jesus had to learn many things, like how to hold a cup, how to talk, and how to count. He learned things from his parents and went to school to learn, too. But though Jesus was a real human being, he never did anything wrong—he never sinned—like stealing, lying, disobeying his parents, or saying bad words. Sometimes Jesus did things that *others* said were bad—like helping certain people and speaking out against wrong. But Jesus always did what was right—he always obeyed God.

KEY VERSES: *This suffering is all part of the work God has given you. Christ, who suffered for you, is your example. Follow in his steps. He never sinned. He never told a lie. He never answered back when insulted. When he suffered he did not threaten to get even. He left his case in the hands of God who always judges fairly. (1 Peter 2:21-23)*

RELATED VERSES: *Luke 2:41-51; Hebrews 5:9; 1 Peter 1:18-19*

RELATED QUESTIONS: *Did Jesus ever fight with his brothers? Did Jesus go to school?*

Q: IF JESUS DIED ON THE CROSS, HOW CAN HE BE ALIVE TODAY?

32

A: Jesus lived as a real human being. Jesus' death was a real death, too (he really died on the cross)—the people who killed him made sure of that. When Jesus was killed, all of his followers were very sad. Jesus' body was put in a grave. But three days later, God brought Jesus back to life. Jesus showed his wounds to his disciples. Jesus lives in his special "glorified" body in heaven today. Isn't that great?

KEY VERSES: *I passed on to you from the first what had been told to me. Christ died for our sins just as the Bible said he would. He was buried, and three days later he rose from the grave. This happened just as the prophets said it would. (1 Corinthians 15:3-4)*

RELATED VERSES: *John 20:27; 1 Corinthians 15:12-58*

RELATED QUESTIONS: *Did Jesus really die? Does Jesus still have scrapes and cuts on his body? How did Jesus rise from the dead? Is Jesus invisible now?*

NOTE TO PARENTS: *We call Jesus' postresurrection body a "glorified" body. Jesus was recognized by the disciples, and he ate a meal with them. But he also was able to appear suddenly in their midst—he wasn't limited by space and time. We really don't know anything more about what his body was like or what our body will be like. (See Luke 24:36-43 and John 20:19-31.)*

Q: WHY DO I FEEL AFRAID IF JESUS IS WITH ME?

33

A: Jesus is always with us even though we don't see him and often we don't feel any different. Jesus wants us to learn to trust him, to believe and know that he is there. It's natural to feel afraid. In fact, being afraid can be good. We should be afraid of danger. For example, fear can keep us a safe distance from a mean dog or something else that might hurt us. God wants our fears to remind us to trust him. Being afraid should be a signal to trust God and do what he wants us to do. But it doesn't mean that Jesus isn't with us.

KEY VERSE: *May the Lord of peace himself give you his peace no matter what happens. The Lord be with you all. (2 Thessalonians 3:16)*

RELATED VERSES: *Matthew 28:20; Philippians 4:6*

Q: HOW DID JESUS WALK ON WATER?

34

A: Jesus did a lot of miracles. We don't know how he did them. Jesus is God, so he can do anything. Walking on the water was not Jesus' ordinary way of getting around. He did this miracle, like other miracles, to teach his disciples and to show them his power. Jesus is Lord of the laws of the universe—he's in charge of the water, too, so he can walk on it whenever he wants to.

KEY VERSES: *That evening his disciples went down to the shore to wait for him. Darkness fell and Jesus still hadn't come back. So they got into the boat and headed out across the lake toward Capernaum. But soon a storm swept down upon them as they rowed. The sea grew very rough. And they were in the middle of the lake. Suddenly they saw Jesus walking toward the boat! They were terrified. So he called out to them and told them not to be afraid. Then they were willing to let him come to them. And suddenly the boat was already at the place where they were going! (John 6:16-21)*

RELATED VERSES: *Matthew 14:23-32; Mark 4:35-41; 6:45-51*

NOTE TO PARENTS: *Lots of well-meaning people have tried to explain miracles (such as Jesus' walking on the water) to make them believable to children. But this is a tragic mistake. The fact that miracles are incredible is exactly the point—they show us that God is awesome and powerful.*

Q: WHY DID JESUS DRESS SO FUNNY?

35

A: The clothes worn by Jesus and his followers may look different to us today, but they were in style back then. Jesus wore what people wore at that time. His clothes fit the climate and culture of the day. No one who lived in Jesus' time told him that he dressed funny, and they should know.

KEY VERSES: *So the soldiers crucified Jesus. Then they put his clothes into four piles. There was one piece of clothing for each of them. But they said, "Let's not tear up his robe," for it was seamless. "Let's throw dice to see who gets it." This fulfilled the Scriptures. It said, "They divided my clothes among them and cast lots for my robe." (John 19:23-24)*

RELATED VERSES: *Psalm 22:18; Matthew 27:35*

NOTE TO PARENTS: *Children get their idea of how Jesus dressed from Bible and Sunday school art. This is what we think Jesus might have looked like, but we have no pictures or descriptions of his physical appearance, so we don't know exactly what he looked like.*

Q: WHY DID THEY BEAT UP JESUS?

36

A: Some people got very angry at Jesus because he was speaking against the bad things they were doing. They tried to get Jesus to do what they wanted. Instead, Jesus did what God wanted him to do, and he told everybody how bad those people were. Finally the people got so angry at Jesus that they wanted to kill him. And eventually, that's what they did.

KEY VERSES: *Then the Roman soldiers took him into the barracks of the palace. They called out the whole palace guard. They dressed him in a purple robe. And they made a crown of sharp thorns and put it on his head. Then they cheered, yelling, "Yea! King of the Jews!" They beat him on the head with a cane and spat on him. They made fun of him by bowing down to "worship" him. (Mark 15:16-19)*

RELATED VERSES: *Isaiah 53:4-10; Matthew 26:57-68; Mark 15:15; John 15:14-18*

RELATED QUESTIONS: *Why did they put a thorny crown on Jesus? If Jesus was such a good man, why were people mad at him?*

Q: WHY DID GOD LET THEM HURT JESUS?

37

A: When Jesus was being hurt, he could have called on angels to save him. After all, he was God's Son. But Jesus chose to suffer and die *for us*. Jesus loved us so much that he did what it took to pay for our sins. Jesus and the Father agreed that it was necessary for him to die on the cross.

KEY VERSES: *He has so much kindness! He took away all our sins through the blood of his Son. This saved us. He has showered upon us the richness of his grace. He understands us and knows what is best for us at all times. God has told us his secret reason for sending Christ. He has a plan he decided on in mercy long ago. He plans to gather us all together when the time is ripe. He will gather his people in Heaven and on earth. They will be with him in Christ forever. (Ephesians 1:7-10)*

RELATED VERSES: *Matthew 26:53; 27:46; 1 John 2:2*

RELATED QUESTION: *Why didn't Jesus save himself from dying on the cross?*

Q: WHY DO THEY CALL IT GOOD FRIDAY IF THAT'S THE DAY JESUS DIED?

38

A: The day Jesus died is called "Good Friday" because it was a good day for us—Jesus died for us, in our place. That day was both a happy day and a sad day. It was sad because Jesus suffered and died. But it was happy because Jesus paid the penalty for our sins. At the time, the day was not seen as Good Friday. But by Easter morning, after Jesus had been raised from the dead, everybody knew it was good.

KEY VERSES: *He was taken out of the city. He carried his cross to the place known as "The Skull." In Hebrew it was called "Golgotha." There they crucified him and two others with him. One was on either side, with Jesus between them. (John 19:17-18)*

RELATED VERSES: *Matthew 27:32–28:20; Mark 15:16-47; Luke 23:26-56*

Q: WHY DOES JESUS WANT US TO FOLLOW HIM?

39

A: Jesus told the people to follow him because he is the way to God, heaven, and eternal life. When Jesus was on earth, the disciples and others followed him by walking close to him and listening to his words. Today, we follow Jesus by copying his example and by doing what he says.

KEY VERSES: *Then Jesus said to the disciples, "Do you want to be my followers? If you do, you must deny yourselves. You must take up your cross and follow me. For anyone who keeps his life for himself shall lose it. And anyone who loses his life for me shall find it again. What good is it if you gain the whole world and lose eternal life? What could ever be as good as eternal life?" (Matthew 16:24-26)*

RELATED VERSES: *Matthew 4:19; John 14:6*

Q: WHY DID JESUS GET TEMPTED BY THE DEVIL?

40

A: When someone tempts you, that person is trying to get you to do something. Because Satan is against Jesus, he tried to get Jesus to do something wrong, to sin. But Jesus didn't give in—he didn't sin. Being tempted isn't sin; giving in to temptation is.

KEY VERSES: *This High Priest of ours understands how weak we are. He had the same temptations we do. But he never once gave way to them and sinned. So let us come boldly to the throne of God. There he will give us his mercy. And there we will find grace to help in times of need. (Hebrews 4:15-16)*

RELATED VERSES: *Matthew 4:1-11; Mark 1:12-13; Luke 4:1-13*

RELATED QUESTION: *What does "being tempted" mean?*

Q: WHY DIDN'T GOD JUST FORGIVE EVERYBODY?

41

A: It would not be right or fair for God to just forgive everyone. There is a penalty that must be paid for doing wrong. The penalty for sinning against God is death, eternal death. But God loved us so much that he sent Jesus, his only Son, to pay our penalty. Jesus did this by dying on the cross, in our place. Now everyone can be forgiven by trusting in Christ.

KEY VERSES: *Yes, all have sinned. All fall short of God's perfect glory. But if we trust in Jesus Christ, God says we are "not guilty." In his kindness he freely takes away our sins. God sent Christ Jesus to take the punishment for our sins. He ended all God's anger against us. Christ's blood and our faith saves us from God's anger. This is the way he could be fair to everybody. He did not punish the people who sinned before Christ came. He was looking forward to the time when Christ would come and take away those sins. (Romans 3:23-25)*

RELATED VERSES: *Mark 8:31; John 3:16; Romans 5:8; Hebrews 2:14-17; 8:3; 9:13-14, 22-23; 1 John 1:7*

RELATED QUESTION: *Why did Jesus have to die?*

SALVATION

Q: WHY DO GOD AND JESUS LOVE PEOPLE?

42

A: God loves us because that's what he decided to do. God doesn't love us because we're good or nice people. In fact, no one could ever be good enough to be worthy of God's love. Isn't it amazing that God loves us even though we sometimes ignore him and disobey him?

KEY VERSE: *But God showed his great love for us. He sent Christ to die for us while we were still sinners. (Romans 5:8)*

RELATED VERSES: *John 1:12; 16:7*

NOTE TO PARENTS: *The best way to help children understand God's love is to demonstrate it to them. Hug them, train them, cheer them, guide them, discipline them, talk to them, spend time with them, accept them, forgive them, help them, stand by them, and provide for them— then they'll understand.*

Q: HOW CAN JESUS FIT IN MY HEART?

43

A: When we say "heart," we mean deep down inside us—where we really feel and believe. So when someone says, "Jesus lives in my heart," the person means that he has asked Jesus to be his Savior—to forgive and take care of him—and that Jesus is in charge of his life. When someone asks Jesus to take over, God really does come inside—the Holy Spirit comes and lives inside that person. And the Holy Spirit can be in all of the people who love God at the same time. Jesus wants to be very close to you, too, like a good friend. Through his Holy Spirit, he wants to "live in your heart."

KEY VERSES: *He has kept this secret for centuries and generations past. But now he is pleased to tell it to the brothers and sisters. The riches and glory of his plan are for you Gentiles, too. This is the secret: Christ in your hearts is your only hope of glory. (Colossians 1:26-27)*

RELATED VERSES: *John 16:7-8; Acts 1:8; 1 Thessalonians 4:8*

RELATED QUESTION: *How can other people have Jesus in their hearts if he's in mine?*

NOTE TO PARENTS: *Children are often told that Jesus comes to live inside their hearts when they believe in him. Young children take this literally and think that a miniaturized Jesus actually lives in their chest. "Jesus lives in my heart" is a shorthand way of calling Jesus Savior and Lord. "Jesus goes with you everywhere" may be a better way of phrasing it for young children.*

Q: HOW DO YOU GET JESUS IN YOUR HEART?

44

A: You become a Christian by asking Jesus to take over your life. You know that you have done wrong things, that you have sinned, and you recognize that you need Jesus to forgive your sins. So you tell Jesus about your sins and that you are sorry, and you ask for his forgiveness. Then you do what Jesus says.

KEY VERSES: *But now God has shown us another way to Heaven. It is not by "being good enough" and trying to keep his laws. It is by a new way. It is not really new. Because the Scriptures told about it long ago. Now God says he will accept us and declare us "not guilty." He will do this if we trust Jesus Christ to take away our sins. We all can be saved by coming to Christ. It doesn't matter who we are or what we have been like. Yes, all have sinned. All fall short of God's perfect glory. But if we trust in Jesus Christ, God says we are "not guilty." In his kindness he freely takes away our sins. (Romans 3:21-24)*

RELATED VERSES: *John 5:24; Acts 19:18; 1 John 1:9*

RELATED QUESTION: *How does someone become a Christian?*

Q: WOULD GOD SEND NICE PEOPLE TO HELL IF THEY ARE NOT CHRISTIANS?

45

A: Compared to each other, some people are nice and some are mean. But compared to God, all people are not very good. All people need to be forgiven for their sins, not just "mean people." To be fair, God has to punish sin. God doesn't *want* to send anyone to hell. That's why he sent Jesus—to pay the penalty for our sins by dying on the cross. But, unfortunately, not all people are willing to admit that they sin and ask for forgiveness. They don't accept the payment of Jesus' death for them. So God lets them experience the results of their choice.

KEY VERSES: *The Bible says, "No one is good without God. Every person in the world has sinned." No one has ever really followed God's paths or even truly wanted to. Everyone has turned away from God. All have gone wrong. No one anywhere has kept on doing what is right. (Romans 3:10-12)*

RELATED VERSES: *Romans 5:16; Jude 1:4*

RELATED QUESTION: *Who will God send to hell?*

Q: IF I SWEAR, WILL I GO TO HELL WHEN I DIE?

46

A: Although it is very important to watch what we say, God doesn't decide who goes to hell because of our speech. Instead, our forgiveness and eternal life are based on the death and resurrection of Jesus Christ. If we trust Jesus to save us, we are forgiven. Of course that doesn't make it all right to swear. We should always try to speak and do what is right.

KEY VERSES: *Because of his kindness, you have been saved through trusting Christ. And even that trust is not your own. It, too, is a gift from God. Salvation is not a reward for the good we have done. So none of us can take any credit for it. (Ephesians 2:8-9)*

RELATED VERSES: *Romans 3:14; James 3:10*

RELATED QUESTION: *What happens to people who use bad words?*

NOTE TO PARENTS: *Many children think they are too bad or evil to be forgiven by God. If you sense that your child feels this way, he or she needs to know that God can forgive any sin. Tell your children that they are not uniquely bad—all people sin.*

Q: WILL ALL OF MY FRIENDS GO TO HEAVEN?

47

A: God loves your friends just as he loves you. Only God knows who will go to heaven and hell; we don't. But there is only one way to heaven—through Jesus. So we can go to heaven only if we have given our life to Christ. If your friends don't follow Jesus, you can help them understand by telling them the Good News about Jesus and how he died for them. Heaven is worth going to even if your friends don't. There will be no good times in hell.

KEY VERSE: *Jesus said, "I am the Way, the Truth, and the Life. No one can get to the Father except through me." (John 14:6)*

RELATED VERSES: *John 5:24; 11:25; Acts 4:12; 1 John 2:23*

RELATED QUESTION: *Does God love my friends?*

NOTE TO PARENTS: *This may be a good opportunity to encourage your child to invite a friend to church or Sunday school.*

Q: WHY ISN'T EVERYONE A CHRISTIAN?

48

A: Not everyone wants to be a Christian, and God doesn't force people to follow Jesus. Some people don't just reject Christ, they also act mean to Christians. That's because they don't understand the love that God has for them. We should try to tell these people about God's love for them.

KEY VERSES: *[Jesus is praying] "And now I am coming to you. I have told them many things while I was with them. They should be filled with my joy. I have given them your commands. And the world hates them. This is because they don't belong in the world, just as I don't. I'm not asking you to take them out of the world. I am asking that you keep them from the evil one. They are not part of this world any more than I am." (John 17:13-16)*

RELATED VERSES: *Matthew 7:14; John 15:9*

RELATED QUESTION: *Why do some people laugh when I talk about Jesus?*

NOTE TO PARENTS: *You can pray with your child for others to become Christians.*

Q: WHY DOESN'T GOD JUST ZAP THE BAD PEOPLE?

49

A: God loves people so much, even the worst people in the world, that he is giving them time to turn away from being bad and to turn to him. God is very patient. Someday, however, the time will be up, and all those who refuse to live God's way and give their lives to Christ will be punished. That will be a very sad day, but it will come.

KEY VERSE: *It may seem like he is slow in coming back as he promised. But he isn't. He is waiting because he does not want anyone to die. He is giving more time for sinners to repent. (2 Peter 3:9)*

RELATED VERSES: *Matthew 13:24-30; Hebrews 10:23*

RELATED QUESTION: *Why do people get away with being bad?*

Q: HOW LONG IS ETERNITY?

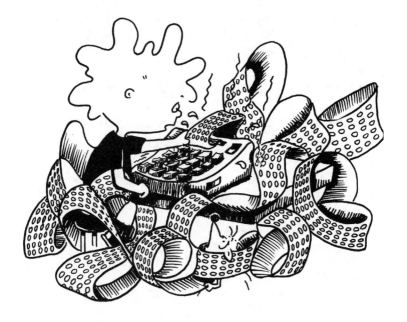

50

A: We can't even imagine how long eternity is. Eternity goes on forever. Sometimes we have good times that we wish would never end—such as a party or a vacation or a visit by a friend from out of town. But they do come to an end. Eternity, however, never ends. God is eternal, and he has given us eternal life. If we know Jesus, we will live forever with him, someday in heaven, after our life on earth comes to an end.

KEY VERSE: *But don't forget this, dear friends! A day is like 1,000 years to the Lord. (2 Peter 3:8)*

RELATED VERSES: *Psalm 41:13; 90:4; 1 Timothy 1:17*

RELATED QUESTION: *What is eternity?*

Q: WHAT DOES GOD WANT US TO DO?

51

A: In the Bible, God's Word, God tells us what he wants us to do, how he wants us to live. Although there are a lot of messages and information in the Bible, God's four main instructions for our lives are: (1) believe in Jesus and trust him every day; (2) obey Jesus and do what he says; (3) love God and others; (4) be fair and honest and live for God without being proud about it.

KEY VERSES: *They replied, "What should we do to satisfy God?" Jesus told them, "God's will is that you believe in the one he has sent." (John 6:28-29)*

RELATED VERSES: *Ecclesiastes 12:13-14; Micah 6:6-8; Matthew 19:19; 22:39*

RELATED QUESTION: *How can I know what God wants me to do?*

PRAYER

Q: IF GOD GIVES US EVERYTHING
WE ASK FOR, THEN HOW COME
WE DON'T HAVE EVERYTHING?

52

A: God doesn't give us everything we *ask* for. He gives us everything we *need,* when we need it. Sometimes we want things that could hurt us, such as when a baby wants to play in the fire. God knows what can hurt us, so he doesn't give us those things because he loves us. God wants to give us what is good for us.

KEY VERSE: *When you do ask you don't get it because your whole aim is wrong. You want only what will make you happy. (James 4:3)*

RELATED VERSES: *Matthew 7:7-11; 21:22; Luke 11:9*

RELATED QUESTION: *Why didn't I get what I prayed for?*

NOTE TO PARENTS: *If your child is older, you may want to explain that there are three types of pray-ers: (1) those who don't ask, (2) those who ask with the wrong motives, and (3) those who consider what God wants and pray accordingly. This question may be a chance to find a need that your child has and pray with him or her about it.*

Q: WHY DO WE PRAY?

53

A: Prayer is talking with God. When we have a good friend, we talk to that person about all sorts of things. That's part of being a friend. In the same way, we should talk to God about what is happening in our life. God wants us to share our life with him, to tell him about what makes us happy, sad, and afraid. He wants to know what we want and what we would like him to do, for ourself and for others. Also, when we pray, we open ourself up to God so that he can make good changes in us.

KEY VERSES: *Don't worry about anything. Instead, pray about everything. Tell God your needs, and don't forget to thank him for his answers. If you do this, you will find God's peace. It is far more wonderful than the human mind can understand. God's peace will keep your thoughts and your hearts as you trust in Christ Jesus. (Philippians 4:6-7)*

RELATED VERSES: *Luke 6:12; Acts 6:1-4; Ephesians 6:12-13; James 4:2*

RELATED QUESTION: *What is prayer?*

NOTE TO PARENTS: Practical Christianity *(LaVonne Neff and others, Tyndale House Publishers) and* What Is Prayer? *(Carolyn Nystrom, Moody Press) are two good resources for more on the topic of prayer.*

Q: WILL GOD GIVE CHILDREN TOYS IF THEY ASK HIM FOR THEM?

GOD
the real
North Pole

54

A: Some people think God is there to give us toys and other things we want. But God doesn't just hand out stuff to us. His purpose is to make us into people who are like Christ. God really cares about us, and he knows what we need. Although toys seem important sometimes, there are other things that we need more. God also doesn't want us to get our happiness from toys, but from him and from other people.

KEY VERSES: *You want what you don't have. So you kill to get it! You long for what others have. So you start a fight to take it away! Why don't you have what you want? Because you don't ask God for it. When you do ask you don't get it because your whole aim is wrong. You want only what will make you happy. (James 4:2-3)*

RELATED VERSES: *Philippians 4:4-10; 1 Thessalonians 5:17*

RELATED QUESTIONS: *If I pray for something, will God give it to me? Does God care about me?*

Q: WHAT SHOULD I SAY TO GOD WHEN I PRAY?

55

A: When we pray, it's easy to say the same words over and over. Prayer can become a habit that we don't think about. Instead, we should think about what we are saying when we pray, and we should be honest with God. Also, we shouldn't pray to show off, but we should say to God what we want to tell him. The Lord's Prayer can be a guide for what to talk to God about. Prayers can include thanking God for who he is and for what he has done. In prayer we can confess our sins, telling God that we are sorry for the bad things we have done. We can make requests, too, asking God to help others and to give us strength and guidance. We can talk to God about anything on our mind.

KEY VERSES: *[Jesus is speaking] "Pray like this: 'Our Father in Heaven, we honor your holy name. We ask that your kingdom will come now. May your will be done here on earth, just as it is in Heaven. Give us our food again today, as usual. And forgive us our sins, just as we have forgiven those who have sinned against us. Don't bring us into temptation. But keep us safe from the Evil One. Amen.'" (Matthew 6:9-13)*

RELATED VERSES: *Luke 11:1-13; Philippians 4:6; 1 Thessalonians 5:17; 1 Timothy 2:8; James 5:16*

NOTE TO PARENTS: *Children can get caught into a routine prayer. Look for ways to vary the family prayers in which your children participate. For example, you could suggest that each member of the family pray about what happened during the day, or you could compile a family prayer list and use it to guide your family prayer times.*

Q: HOW COME WHEN I PRAY TO GOD HE DOESN'T ALWAYS ANSWER?

Hello—you've reached heaven's 1-800 number. There isn't anyone here to take your call right now, but if you leave a long message at the sound of the choir, we will return your call. This is a recording...

56

A: There's a difference between hearing and answering. God hears all our prayers, but he doesn't always give us what we ask for. Also, he answers all our prayers, but not always the way we want him to. When we ask God for something, sometimes he answers no or wait. A good answer is not always yes.

KEY VERSES: *Yes, the Lord hears the good man when he calls for help. He saves him out of all his troubles. The Lord is close to those whose hearts are breaking. He saves those who are sorry for their sins. The good man does not escape all troubles. But the Lord helps him in each and every one. (Psalm 34:17-19)*

RELATED VERSES: *Psalm 139:4; 2 Corinthians 12:8; 1 Peter 5:7*

RELATED QUESTION: *Does God always hear my prayers?*

Q: WHY DID I HAVE A BAD DREAM WHEN I PRAYED BEFORE I WENT TO SLEEP?

57

A: It's good to pray before falling asleep at night. Praying helps us think through the day and thank God for how much he loves us. We should also pray for the next day. Christians aren't promised that they will be free from all problems and difficulties. God does promise to be with us during hard times. A lot of things can cause bad dreams—something on our mind, something we ate, a noise. Ask God to help you sleep, but remember that whatever happens, he is there with you.

KEY VERSE: *Then I lay down and slept in peace and woke up safely. For the Lord was watching over me. (Psalm 3:5)*

RELATED VERSES: *Psalm 34:17-19; 139:7-11; Proverbs 3:24-26; Matthew 2:12-13; Acts 2:17*

RELATED QUESTION: *If God is with me, why did he let me have a bad dream?*

Q: HOW CAN GOD HEAR EVERYONE'S PRAYERS AT ONCE?

58

A: God can hear everyone's prayers at once because God is everywhere. We can only be in one place at a time, and usually we can't understand more than one person at a time. But God is not like us—he is not limited. Not only can God hear and understand everyone who is praying to him in many different languages, but he also can give each person his full attention. Isn't that great?

KEY VERSES: *[God is speaking] "Am I a God who is only in one place? Do they think I cannot see what they are doing? Can anyone hide from me? Am I not everywhere in Heaven and earth at the same time?" (Jeremiah 23:23-24)*

RELATED VERSES: *Luke 1:13; Acts 10:31*

RELATED QUESTION: *How can God hear people praying at the same time from different countries?*

NOTE TO PARENTS: *Many children harbor the misconception that God is limited as we are. This is partly unavoidable because children think concretely. But it is also an opportunity for you to introduce them to the idea that God is infinitely greater than we are. He can even hear thousands of prayers at once! An illustration that might help: When five people touch you, you can feel all five.*

HEAVEN

AND

HELL

Q: IF WE WENT HIGH ENOUGH IN THE SKY, WOULD WE FIND HEAVEN?

59

A: No one but God knows exactly where heaven is. But the best way we can describe its location is to say it is "up." If we rode a spaceship up, way out into space, we would not find heaven—it can't be seen or found by people. Only God can take us there. And that's what he does, after we die, if we have trusted in Jesus as our Savior.

KEY VERSES: *Not long after this, Jesus rose into the sky. He went up into a cloud, leaving them staring after him. They were straining their eyes for another look at him. But suddenly two white-robed men were standing there with them. They said, "Men of Galilee, why are you standing here staring at the sky? Jesus has gone to Heaven. And someday he will come back again, just as he went!" (Acts 1:9-11)*

RELATED VERSES: *John 3:13; Luke 24:50-51*

RELATED QUESTIONS: *Where is heaven? Is heaven up?*

Q: WHAT IS HEAVEN LIKE?

60

A: The Bible uses some wonderful pictures to tell us what heaven is like. In our world, we think that gold is important because it's so valuable. But in heaven, the streets will be gold—we'll *walk* on it. The best way to picture heaven is to imagine the most exciting and fun place that you've ever been to. Heaven will be like that only much, much better. Jesus told his followers that he was leaving earth to go to heaven to prepare a place for them. He has a special place for us, where there is no crying or sadness and we will be filled with joy.

KEY VERSES: *[Jesus is speaking] "There are many homes in my Father's house. I am going to prepare a place for you. I will come again and take you to me. Then you will be with me where I am about to go. If this weren't so, I would tell you plainly." (John 14:2-3)*

RELATED VERSES: *Isaiah 60:17; Revelation 21:21*

RELATED QUESTIONS: *What will we do in heaven? Are the streets in heaven real gold or just painted gold?*

Q: IS THERE A McDONALD'S IN HEAVEN?

HEAVEN
FROM JASON'S
PERSPECTIVE

Fly-Thru

61

A: No. In heaven, we won't need people to work to make us food. Our bodies will be different. They will be "glorified," or perfect, bodies. We don't know if we will eat there or what kind of food we will need. God will make sure that we have everything we need. Heaven will be fun. It will be great!

KEY VERSES: *[When Jesus appeared to the disciples] Still they stood there, unsure. They were filled with joy and doubt. Then he asked them, "Do you have anything here to eat?" They gave him a piece of broiled fish. And he ate it as they watched! (Luke 24:41-43)*

RELATED VERSES: *Romans 16:18; Philippians 3:19*

RELATED QUESTIONS: *What do we eat in heaven? Are there going to be things I enjoy in heaven? Is there school in heaven?*

NOTE TO PARENTS: *Children are concerned about food. Food is important to them, and they don't want to be hungry. Curiosity about what they will be eating in heaven may underlie questions like these.*

Q: WILL THERE BE TOYS IN HEAVEN?

62

A: We like toys because we have such fun with them. But we can get tired of toys, too. For example, you don't play with your baby toys any more. That's because you outgrew them and got tired of them. God will have just the right kind of toys for you in heaven. You will enjoy heaven even more than your favorite toys.

KEY VERSES: *When I was a child I thought like a child does. When I became a man I put away the childish things. We can see and understand only a little about God now. It is like we were looking at his reflection in a poor mirror. Someday we are going to see him face to face. Now all that I know is hazy and blurred. But then I will see everything clearly. I will see as clearly as God sees into my heart right now. (1 Corinthians 13:11-12)*

RELATED VERSES: *Ephesians 4:14; 1 Corinthians 14:20*

RELATED QUESTIONS: *Will I have my teddy bear in heaven? Do toys go to heaven?*

Q: WILL MY PET GO TO HEAVEN WHEN IT DIES?

63

A: We don't know what happens to animals when they die, but God does, and we know his plan is good. Sometimes we may get the idea that animals think and understand as we do. But God created animals different from people. Animals don't have souls or think as we do, so they can't enjoy God the way we can. Here on earth, pets are fun to play with and animals are interesting to watch. Only God knows if pets will join us in heaven.

KEY VERSES: *God made all sorts of wild animals and cattle and reptiles. And God was pleased with what he had done. Then God said, "Let us make a man—someone like ourselves. He will be the master of all life upon the earth and in the skies and in the seas." So God made man like his Maker. Like God did God make man. Man and maid did he make them. (Genesis 1:25-27)*

RELATED VERSES: *Isaiah 11:6-8; 65:25*

RELATED QUESTION: *Where do animals go when they die?*

NOTE TO PARENTS: *This question may be a way of testing the reality of heaven. A child's world is tied to his or her pet, and the death of a pet naturally raises the question of what happens to it afterward. But if you're not sure how to answer, don't be afraid of saying you don't know. The answer may not be as important as helping your child deal with losing a pet. When we get to heaven, God will give us everything we need to be filled with unspeakable joy.*

Q: WHY CAN'T WE GO TO HEAVEN AND JUST SEE IT AND THEN COME BACK?

64

A: This question is like asking, "Can I become a teenager and then come back to my age right now?" It's impossible because you have to *grow* into your teens; you can't simply jump there and back. In the same way, heaven is more than a place you can visit. It's a time at the end of life, and God has to make us ready to go there. In fact, we have to change in order to go there. We know that heaven exists because God has told us so in his Word, the Bible. And Jesus promised to "prepare a place" so that we can live with him forever (John 14:2). Once we get there, we won't want to come back.

KEY VERSES: *Then I looked and saw a door standing open in Heaven. I heard the same voice I had heard before. It was the one that sounded like a mighty trumpet blast. It said, "Come up! I will show you what must happen in the future!" And instantly I was in the spirit. And I saw a throne and someone sitting on it! Great bursts of light flashed forth from him. It was like light from a glittering diamond or from a shining ruby. There was a rainbow glowing like an emerald around his throne. (Revelation 4:1-3)*

RELATED VERSES: *Exodus 33:22; Matthew 17:2; 2 Corinthians 12:2-3*

RELATED QUESTIONS: *Is heaven really there? Why can't I go to heaven now? How do we get to heaven after we die?*

Q: WILL I HAVE MY SAME NAME IN HEAVEN?

65

A: When we get to heaven, we will see our friends and family members who have died and gone there before us. They will recognize us, and we will know them. The Bible says that when we trust Christ as Savior, our names are written in the "Book of Life." That's God's list of who gets into heaven.

KEY VERSE: *[Jesus is speaking] "All who conquer will be dressed in white. I will not erase their names from the Book of Life. I will announce before my Father and his angels that they are mine." (Revelation 3:5)*

RELATED VERSES: *Isaiah 62:1-3; Luke 16:19-24*

RELATED QUESTIONS: *Will people know me in heaven? Will I remember my family and friends in heaven? Will life in heaven be like it is here? Will I stay the same in heaven as I am here?*

Q: WILL GOD LET ME VISIT GRANDPA IN HEAVEN?

66

A: One of the great things about going to heaven is getting to see the people we love and want to see. If those people have trusted in Christ, they will be there. If your grandpa is in heaven, you will be able to see him when you go there.

KEY VERSES: *The believers who are dead will be the first to rise to meet the Lord. Then we who are alive and remain on the earth will be caught up with them. We will go to the clouds to meet the Lord in the air. We will stay with him forever. So comfort and cheer each other with this news. (1 Thessalonians 4:16-18)*

RELATED VERSES: *Daniel 7:13; Matthew 17:1-3; Acts 7:56*

RELATED QUESTION: *Why did God take Grandpa to heaven?*

NOTE TO PARENTS: *If a grandparent has died recently, your child will have many questions like this one. He or she may also want to express grief over the loss. Be open to talk to your child about his or her feelings.*

Q: WHY IS HELL DARK IF THEY HAVE FIRES?

67

A: The Bible uses a lot of pictures to give us an idea of what heaven and hell are like. Fire means burning and pain. Do you remember having a fever? You felt like you were burning up, but there was no flame. Darkness means loneliness. Can you imagine anything more lonely than sitting by yourself in total darkness? What God is telling us is that hell is a terrible place. We certainly don't want to go there.

KEY VERSE: *[Jesus is speaking] "And many . . . shall be thrown into outer darkness. They will be put in the place of crying and pain." (Matthew 8:12)*

RELATED VERSES: *Luke 16:28; Revelation 20:15*

RELATED QUESTIONS: *What's really happening in hell? What is hell like?*

NOTE TO PARENTS: *Children hear conflicting descriptions of hell. They hear that hell is a dark place (Matthew 8:12) and yet a lake of fire (Revelation 19:20). (They may also have heard that it is cold.) Instead of grasping the meanings of these metaphors, the child is taking the images concretely.*

Q: WHO ENDS UP IN HELL?

68

A: Hell is the place where God will punish Satan and his followers—and all those who refuse to follow God. We don't know exactly who will go there because we don't make that judgment, God does. But God has made it possible for everyone to escape punishment in hell. He gives everyone the opportunity to go to heaven. That's why he sent Jesus to die on the cross. When Jesus suffered and died, he took our place—he paid the penalty for our sins. So if we trust in Jesus, we can escape hell and go to heaven. It sure would be great if all our friends, family, and neighbors would end up in heaven. Let's tell them how to get there.

KEY VERSE: *Anyone whose name wasn't in the Book of Life was thrown into the Lake of Fire. (Revelation 20:15)*

RELATED VERSES: *John 3:16-18; 1 John 1:9*

RELATED QUESTIONS: *Are there kids in hell? Who goes to hell? Will I go to hell if I swear?*

ANGELS
AND
DEMONS

Q: WHAT DO ANGELS REALLY LOOK LIKE?

69

A: The word *angel* means "messenger." Angels are God's messengers. They can also be God's warriors. In the Bible we read about people who saw angels. Sometimes the people knew they were angels, and sometimes they didn't. Some angels described in the Bible have wings. Those angels are called cherubim. But most of the angels in the Bible stories looked like regular people. We don't know what angels look like in heaven.

KEY VERSES: *I, John, saw and heard all these things. I fell down to worship the angel who showed them to me. But he said, "No, don't do anything like that. I am a servant of Jesus like you, and like your brothers the prophets. I am like all those who hear and act on the truth stated in this book. Only worship God." (Revelation 22:8-9)*

RELATED VERSES: *Genesis 19:1; Hebrews 13:2*

RELATED QUESTIONS: *Are angels boys or girls? Do angels eat?*

NOTE TO PARENTS: *You may want to ask if your child has seen a picture of an angel, perhaps in a children's Bible, in a painting, in the cartoons, etc. Those pictures often leave mental impressions about an angel's appearance.*

Q: WHEN I DIE, WILL I BECOME AN ANGEL?

70

A: Angels are spiritual beings created by God. They are different from human beings. You are a spiritual being, too. In other words, you have a soul and will live forever and can know God. But you are also a physical being. You live on earth and have a physical body. When you die, you will leave your physical body behind and will be given a glorified or perfect body in heaven. We don't know exactly what our glorified bodies will be like, but we know that people in heaven will be able to recognize us. One thing is for sure, we don't become angels when we die. In fact, angels will serve us in heaven. Wow!

KEY VERSE: *Don't you know that we will judge the angels in Heaven? You should be able to decide your problems here on earth easily enough. (1 Corinthians 6:3)*

RELATED VERSES: *Psalm 8:5; Hebrews 2:7*

RELATED QUESTIONS: *How many angels are there? Do you have to die to be a spirit?*

NOTE TO PARENTS: *According to Matthew 26:53 and other passages, there are thousands of angels.*

Q: WHAT DOES MY ANGEL DO?

71

A: Angels are God's helpers. They live in heaven with him. God often instructs angels to protect people by blocking the evil that Satan directs at them. Angels also carry out God's purposes in people's lives. In other words, angels help us do what God wants us to do.

KEY VERSE: *[Jesus is speaking] "Be careful that you don't look down upon a single one of these children. For I tell you that in Heaven their angels can speak directly to my Father." (Matthew 18:10)*

RELATED VERSES: *Genesis 24:7; Numbers 22:15-35; Daniel 3:28; 6:22; Matthew 1:21-24; 4:11; Hebrews 1:14*

RELATED QUESTION: *Are there angels in the room with us?*

NOTE TO PARENTS: *Some people think that each person has a guardian angel, an angel assigned to a person to watch over and protect him or her. We don't know for sure if people have guardian angels. But we do know that God uses angels to accomplish his will.*

Q: WHO IS THE DEVIL?

72

A: The devil is also called Satan. The word *devil* means "liar" or "enemy." Satan used to be an angel. But he wanted to be like God, so he fought against God. God kicked him out of heaven. Ever since then, Satan has worked on earth, trying to defeat God and God's people. He is God's enemy. But God is far stronger than Satan. In the end, Satan will be thrown into hell and suffer forever.

KEY VERSE: *But if you keep on sinning, it shows you belong to Satan. He has been sinning from the beginning. But the Son of God came to destroy the works of the devil. (1 John 3:8)*

RELATED VERSES: *Genesis 3:1-15; 1 Chronicles 21:1; Job 1:6-13; 2:1-7; Zechariah 3:1-2; Matthew 4:1-11; John 14:30; 2 Corinthians 11:14; Ephesians 6:11; Hebrews 2:14*

RELATED QUESTIONS: *Why did God make the devil? Why doesn't God kill Satan? Will God forgive Satan?*

Q: DOES THE DEVIL HAVE CLAWS?

73

A: The devil can take many forms. When he tempted Adam and Eve, he was a serpent. But remember, Satan is an angel and once was an angel of light. So he probably doesn't look like the funny costumes we see at Halloween (all red, with horns and a pitchfork). Instead, the devil usually tries to look like something good and beautiful. Remember, Satan is the father of lies, so he is usually trying to trick us. He'll say that we don't deserve to be God's children and that we are not forgiven. But always remember that God is much stronger than Satan (it's not even a close contest), and God can keep us safe from Satan.

KEY VERSE: *Yet I am not surprised! Satan can change himself into an angel of light. (2 Corinthians 11:14)*

RELATED VERSES: *Job 1:6-13; 2:1-7; Luke 11:4; John 8:44; James 4:7*

RELATED QUESTIONS: *Can the devil hurt me? Is the devil more powerful than God?*

NOTE TO PARENTS: *When children hear about Satan, they may wonder if he can hurt them physically. Of course that's possible, but Satan's attacks are usually much more subtle and focused on keeping people far from God. Usually he tries to get us to center our life around anything but God and to ignore God's commands. Explain to your child that God beats the devil every time and that we can beat Satan too (resist his temptations) if we stay close to God. This means doing what God says, relying on him, and talking to him about everything in our life.*

ANGELS AND DEMONS

Q: WHY IS THE DEVIL AFTER US?

74

A: Satan is God's enemy, so he is against anyone who is on God's side. Satan is jealous of our friendship with God—he can't stand it when we spend time with the Lord. And he wants to stop us from obeying God and from doing good. The devil hates God, so he hates us because we love God.

KEY VERSE: *So give yourselves humbly to God. Resist the devil and he will run from you. (James 4:7)*

RELATED VERSES: *Ephesians 6:11; 1 Peter 5:8-9; Revelation 12:9*

Q: WHAT ARE DEMONS?

SHHHHHH...
Demon
trapp!

75

A: Like the devil, demons are bad angels. They followed Satan when he turned against God. Demons are spiritual beings who work and fight against God. Demons are Satan's helpers. There is only one devil, but there are thousands of demons. They are all over the world, trying to keep people from following Christ and obeying God. But God is more powerful than all the demons and the devil put together. God will keep us safe from demons as we trust in him. At the end of time, all demons will be thrown into the Lake of Fire with the devil.

KEY VERSE: *[Jesus is speaking] "Then I will turn to those on my left. I will say, 'Away with you, you cursed ones. Go into the fire prepared for the devil and his demons.'"* *(Matthew 25:41)*

RELATED VERSES: *Mark 5:9-13; Luke 4:41; 11:15; Revelation 18:2*

NOTE TO PARENTS: *The related verses show that demons are active in the world.*

Q: WILL I EVER GET A DEMON?

76

A: It's easy to get the idea from watching television and hearing kids talk that demons can take over people's lives whenever they want. But that's not true. It is true that some people have demons in them. But demons can only enter people who let them and who are not close to God. And never forget, God is much more powerful than Satan or any of the demons. He can protect us.

KEY VERSES: *When the 70 disciples came back, they gave [Jesus] a joyful report. They said, "Even the demons obey us when we use your name." "Yes," he told them. "I saw Satan falling from Heaven like a flash of light! I have given you the power to walk among snakes and scorpions. And I have given you authority over the power of the Enemy. Nothing shall hurt you! But don't be full of joy because the demons obey you. Be full of joy because your names are written in Heaven." (Luke 10:17-20)*

RELATED VERSES: *Matthew 10:7-8; Romans 8:38-39*

SUFFERING

AND

EVIL

Q: WHY DO SOME PEOPLE DIE BEFORE THEY ARE OLD?

77

A: Death entered the world when sin came in. Ever since Adam and Eve, pain and death have been part of life. Eventually, everything that is alive in our world has to die. Plants die. Animals die. People die. Death can come from a lot of different causes: automobile accidents, sickness, old age, and so forth. And life is short, no matter how long a person lives. Just ask someone who is sixty or seventy or eighty. Remember that because life is short, we should make the most of every day we are alive. Each breath is a gift from God. But also remember that this life is not all there is. After we die we can live forever with God.

KEY VERSES: *For to me, living is Christ, and dying—well, that's better yet! But if I live I can win people to Christ. So I don't know which is better. Should I live or die? Sometimes I want to live, and at other times I don't. For I long to go and be with Christ. How much happier for me than being here! (Philippians 1:21-23)*

RELATED VERSE: *2 Corinthians 5:6*

Q: WHY ARE SOME PEOPLE DIFFERENT FROM OTHERS?

78

A: Bad things happen in this world, and people suffer. Some people are hurt in accidents. Some are injured in sports. Some are born with physical problems. You can probably think of many ways that people can be harmed. Today there are many doctors, nurses, and other people who can help us when we are hurt or need special help. They can give us medicine and bandages, and they can operate if necessary. And scientists are always working on special tools to help. Glasses, wheel chairs, hearing aids, and artificial legs are just a few of their wonderful inventions. These doctors and scientists are gifts from God.

KEY VERSES: *"Master," [Jesus'] disciples asked him, "why was this man born blind? Was it because of his own sins or those of his parents?" "Neither," Jesus answered. "He was born blind to show the power of God." (John 9:2-3)*

RELATED VERSES: *Matthew 5:4; 2 Corinthians 11:30; 12:8-10; 3 John 1:2*

RELATED QUESTION: *Why does God let people have disabilities?*

NOTE TO PARENTS: *God planned for people to be healthy. Disease, death, and disasters are a result of sin in the world. Everyone living in this sinful world suffers the effects of sin, even Christians. God may allow us to go through difficult times to teach us to rely on him or other lessons. Whatever our struggles, God can be glorified in them. In fact, God delights in demonstrating his strength in weak people.*

Q: HOW COME GOD MAKES STORMS WITH LIGHTENING AND THUNDER?

79

A: God made laws that control how the weather works. Thunder storms are part of our weather. Without rain, the grass, flowers, and crops wouldn't grow. The lightening and thunder in those storms come from the electricity in the air and on the earth. Of course, God can interrupt his laws of nature. But he made those laws so the earth would work. God doesn't send storms to scare us or hurt us. But storms can be dangerous, so we should stay out of their way and find cover when they come.

KEY VERSES: *The clouds poured down their rain. The thunder rolled and crackled in the sky. Your lightning flashed. There was thunder in the whirlwind. The lightning lighted up the world! The earth trembled and shook. (Psalm 77:17-18)*

RELATED VERSES: *1 Kings 18:5-45; Psalm 83:15*

RELATED QUESTIONS: *How come God makes weather hurt people or damage stuff? Does God make the weather every day?*

NOTE TO PARENTS: *As mentioned in the note for question 78, many natural disasters are the result of sin in the world. Of course we don't know all the reasons for hurricanes, earthquakes, tornadoes, and other terrible calamities. But some natural disasters are clearly the result of misusing the environment (for example, strip mining) or poor planning (for example, building on a flood plain).*

Q: WHY DOES GOD LET WARS HAPPEN?

80

A: Wars are a result of sin in the world. Because people aren't perfect, sometimes they get angry and fight. When leaders of countries do this, wars start. Wars are like fights between people, only much, much bigger. If people followed God's instructions for living, there would not be wars. God wants people to get along, not to fight and kill each other. But if we ignore God and break his rules, we suffer. God could stop all wars and fights in the world. But God wants human beings to trust him, to listen to him, to obey him, and to live in peace with each other.

KEY VERSES: *What is causing the fights among you? Isn't it because there is a whole army of evil desires within you? You want what you don't have. So you kill to get it! You long for what others have. So you start a fight to take it away! Why don't you have what you want? Because you don't ask God for it. (James 4:1-2)*

RELATED VERSES: *Matthew 24:6; 1 Corinthians 13:4-8*

RELATED QUESTION: *Does God make bad things happen?*

Q: WHY DOES GOD LET US GET SICK?

81

A: Sometimes sickness is the body's way of telling us that we should stop living a certain way. Perhaps we ate too much (or we ate something bad), or we didn't get enough sleep. Sickness and disease are problems that came into the world with sin. All kinds of people get sick: good and bad, rich and poor, old and young. God wants us to take care of ourself and be healthy so we can live for him. And when we are sick, we can pray to God and ask him to help us.

KEY VERSES: *Is anyone sick? He should call for the elders of the church. They should pray over him and pour a little oil upon him. They should call on the Lord to heal him. If their prayer is offered in faith, it will heal him. The Lord will make him well. If his sickness was caused by some sin, the Lord will forgive him. (James 5:14-15)*

RELATED VERSES: *Romans 5:3; 8:28; 2 Corinthians 12:8-9*

Q: IF WE ARE RUNNING OUT OF TREES, WHY DOESN'T GOD JUST MAKE MORE?

82

A: God *is* making more trees, but it is up to us not to use them faster than he replaces them. Some trees are cut down and used for wood, paper, and other products. Other trees are cut down to make room for houses, shopping centers, roads, and other construction projects. Some people say that we are running out of trees. When God created trees and other plants, he made them with the ability to make new ones. They do this by producing seeds that fall to the ground or are planted and then grow. But it takes many years for a tree to grow to be big and tall. So people should be careful not to cut down more trees than can be replaced by the seeds. God has given human beings the job of taking care of the earth. This includes using the trees wisely and planting new ones.

KEY VERSE: *Then God said, "Let us make a man—someone like ourselves. He will be the master of all life upon the earth and in the skies and in the seas." (Genesis 1:26)*

RELATED VERSES: *Deuteronomy 20:19; Revelation 7:3*

NOTE TO PARENTS: *Faithful stewards of the earth are sensitive to the environment. This kind of question is an opportunity for you to teach your children to take good care of God's earth and its resources.*

Q: DOES GOD KNOW ABOUT PEOPLE WHO ARE HUNGRY?

83

A: God knows everything. He even knows how many hairs you have on your head. God knows about all the hungry people in the world, and it makes him sad. Remember, he put *us* in charge of the world. God wants us to care about people and help those who need it. This includes helping to feed those who are hungry. Think about what you can do to feed the hungry people in your community.

KEY VERSES: *He is the God who made both earth and heaven. He made the seas and all that is in them. He is the God who keeps every promise. He gives justice to the poor. He gives food to the hungry. He sets the prisoners free. (Psalm 146:6-7)*

RELATED VERSES: *Matthew 10:29-31; Acts 27:34*

RELATED QUESTION: *Why doesn't God make enough food for everyone?*

Q: WHY DO BROTHERS AND SISTERS FIGHT?

84

A: Part of what it means to be a human being is to be sinful. In other words, no one in this world is perfect. We all do wrong things—we act in ways that displease God and that get us into trouble. Sinfulness causes us to get on each other's nerves and to get angry with one another. We even argue and fight with people we love, like our parents or our brothers and sisters. God has given us rules for living. If we follow his rules, we will get along with each other.

KEY VERSES: *At harvest time Cain brought the Lord a gift of his farm produce. Abel brought the fatty cuts of meat from his best lambs, and presented them to the Lord. The Lord accepted Abel's offering, but not Cain's. This made Cain dejected and very angry. His face grew dark with fury. "Why are you angry?" the Lord asked him. "Why is your face so dark with rage? It can be bright with joy if you will do what you should! But if you refuse to obey, watch out. Sin is waiting to attack you. It is longing to destroy you. But you can conquer it!" (Genesis 4:3-7)*

RELATED VERSES: *Genesis 4:8; James 4:1*

RELATED QUESTIONS: *Why are some people so mean? Why did God give me mean brothers and sisters?*

Q: WHY DO YOU GET MAD AT ME IF YOU HAVE JESUS IN YOUR HEART?

BIBLE STORIES OF JESUS

85

A: Not all anger is wrong. We should be angry with the bad things in the world, and we should try to make them right. When children disobey their parents and do other things that are wrong, sometimes their parents get angry. Good parents want their children to do what is right, and so they try to teach children right from wrong. Sometimes, of course, parents get angry at children for the wrong reasons. Maybe the parents are grouchy because they've had a bad day. Or maybe they misunderstood what their child did. Parents are human too; they can make mistakes. Even Christian parents who have God living in them and guiding them can do what is wrong at times. That happens when they don't do what God wants them to do. No matter how your parents act, you should love them and pray for them.

KEY VERSE: *If you are angry, don't sin by staying angry. Don't let the sun go down with you still angry. Get over it quickly. (Ephesians 4:26)*

RELATED VERSES: *Ecclesiastes 3:7-8; Romans 7:14; Colossians 3:5-8*

Q: WHAT IS EVIL?

86

A: Evil is another word for what is bad or sinful. Evil is anything that goes against God and displeases him. This includes a selfish attitude, bad actions, and ignoring God. Evil entered the world when Adam and Eve sinned in the Garden of Eden. You can read that story in the book of Genesis in the Bible. Ever since then, humans have been born wanting to do what is wrong. That's called our "sinful nature." So evil in the world comes from sinful human beings doing what comes naturally. Evil also comes directly from Satan. He is the enemy of God. The devil tries to get people to turn against God and disobey him. The good news is that we can overcome evil in ourself and in the world by giving our life to Jesus. God is far greater than Satan.

KEY VERSE: *Keep away from every kind of evil.*
  (1 Thessalonians 5:22)

RELATED VERSES: *Genesis 2:9; Matthew 12:34-35*

RELATED QUESTIONS: *What is sin? How do we displease God?*

THE
BIBLE

Q: HOW DID THEY WRITE THE OLD TESTAMENT IF THERE WEREN'T ANY PAPER OR PENCILS?

87

A: When the oldest books in the Bible were
written, they didn't have typewriters, compu-
ters, or printing presses. And there weren't any ballpoint
pens, felt-tipped pens, or number-two pencils. But the
people who lived back then did have other tools for
writing. The paper they used was different, too. The
paper they first wrote the Old Testament on was probably either *papyrus* or *parchment*. Papyrus paper was
made from a plant that grows in Bible lands. Parchment
was made of animal skin. Either of these could be sewn
into long pieces and rolled up into scrolls. Museums
have some of these ancient scrolls. You may want to visit
a museum and see one.

KEY VERSES: *After the king burned the scroll, the Lord spoke
to Jeremiah. He said, "Get another scroll. Write
everything again just as you did before." (Jeremiah
36:27-28)*

RELATED VERSES: *Exodus 24:12; 2 Timothy 4:13; 2 Peter
1:20-21*

Q: WHO WROTE THE BIBLE?

88

A: The words in the Bible came from God. That's why it is called "God's Word." God used people to write down the ideas, thoughts, teachings, and words that he wanted to put in the Bible. The writers were very special people, chosen by God for this very important task. And God used many people, writing over many, many years. These people wrote in their own style and in their own language, but they wrote God's Word. God guided their thoughts as they wrote. And God made sure that what they wrote was exactly what he wanted. He kept them from making any mistakes. Today we can read the Bible, God's Word, which he wrote through those special people so many years ago.

KEY VERSES: *No prophecy in the Bible was thought up by the prophet himself. The Holy Spirit within these godly men gave them true messages from God. (2 Peter 1:20-21)*

RELATED VERSES: *Exodus 31:18; 2 Timothy 4:13*

RELATED QUESTIONS: *How was the Bible made? Why did God ask certain people to write the Bible?*

89

A: The Bible is true because it is God's Word, and God always speaks the truth. When you read the Bible, you will see that it says it is the Word of God. The Bible also says that every word in it is true. But if that doesn't convince you, read the Bible and see for yourself that everything makes sense. When you read it, you will think, *This sounds right! This is true.* The Bible has also proven to be true over the many hundreds of years since it was written. For example, many events predicted in the Bible have happened, just as it said they would.

KEY VERSE: *The whole Bible was given to us by inspiration from God. It is useful to teach us what is true. It helps us to know what is wrong in our lives. It straightens us out and helps us do what is right. (2 Timothy 3:16)*

RELATED VERSES: *John 10:34-36; Hebrews 4:12; 2 Peter 3:15-16*

RELATED QUESTION: *Did the Bible stories really happen or are they like fairy tales?*

NOTE TO PARENTS: *Children usually will not raise this question as a matter of curiosity until they are older. Most will only ask a question like this if they are (1) mocked for believing the Bible, or (2) don't want to do something God wants them to do. If your children ask it, you might want to probe further before or after answering.*

Q: WHY DO WE HAVE THE BIBLE?

90

A: God gave us the Bible because he wanted to talk to us in a way that we would understand. Because God gave us his Word in a book, we can read it over and over. We can share it with a friend. The Bible is like a map—it shows us the direction to go in life. The Bible is like a love letter—it tells us about God's love for us. The Bible is like food—it gives us strength to live. To find out what God is like and how he wants us to live, read the Bible.

KEY VERSE: *For whatever God says to us is full of living power. It is sharper than the sharpest sword. It cuts swift and deep into our innermost thoughts and desires. It shows us for what we really are. (Hebrews 4:12)*

RELATED VERSES: *John 5:39-40; 16:13-15; 17:20; 20:30-31; Acts 17:11; 2 Timothy 3:16-17*

Q: WHY DO SOME BIBLES HAVE PICTURES AND SOME DON'T?

91

A: The people who wrote the Bible didn't put pictures in them. But in recent years, the people who print Bibles wanted to help us better understand the Bible stories. So they put pictures at various places in the Bible to help us see what Bible people and places may have looked like. The pictures are drawings or paintings, not photographs. These pictures were made recently—they're not very old. The artists knew what to draw by learning about that part of the world and by reading what the Bible says about how people lived in Bible times.

KEY VERSE: *When you come, bring the coat I left at Troas with Carpus. Also bring the books, but especially bring the parchments. (2 Timothy 4:13)*

RELATED VERSES: *2 Timothy 3:16-17*

RELATED QUESTION: *Why are there different Bibles?*

NOTE TO PARENTS: *In the key verse, Paul was in prison, just before his death when he wrote this letter to Timothy. The "parchments" were copies of the Old Testament Scriptures. With this question, children may also be asking why there are different versions of the Bible or why there is a difference between their Bible storybook and your Bible.*

Q: WHEN DID "BIBLE TIMES" STOP?

92

A: The last book in the Bible was written about seventy years after the time Jesus lived on earth. That's a very long time ago, almost two thousand years. In one way that's when Bible times stopped. But in other ways we are still in Bible times. God still speaks to us through his Word, he still cares about us, and he still does miracles. We may not see God divide a sea like he did for Moses, and we may not see anyone walk on water like Jesus did, but God still answers prayer and changes lives.

KEY VERSE: *Tell each other when you do wrong. Pray for each other. Then you will be healed. The earnest prayer of a righteous man has great power and wonderful results. (James 5:16)*

RELATED VERSES: *John 20:30-31; Hebrews 1:1-3; 4:7*

RELATED QUESTIONS: *How long ago was the Bible written? When was the Bible made?*

Q: WHY DID BIBLE PEOPLE GIVE THEIR KIDS SUCH FUNNY NAMES?

93

A: In ancient times, especially among the Jewish people, a person's name was very special. Usually it said something about the person or about the parents' dreams for their child. For example, Jedidiah means "lover of God." Sometimes God told prophets to give their children names with special messages. Hosea named his children Lo-ruhamah and Lo-ammi. Lo-ruhamah means "not loved," and Lo-Ammi means "not my people." By giving his children these unusual names, Hosea was giving God's message to the people. But usually names from other countries and cultures sound strange to us because we're not used to them. Names may sound funny to us, but not to the people in that country. Your name would probably sound funny to the people of Israel.

KEY VERSES: *Soon Gomer had another child. This one was a daughter. And God said to Hosea, "Name her Lo-ruhamah. This means 'No more mercy.' For I will have no more mercy upon Israel. I will not forgive her again. But I will have mercy on the tribe of Judah. I will free her from her enemies. I will do so without any help from her armies or weapons." Once Lo-ruhamah was no longer a baby, Gomer gave birth to a son. And God said, "Call him Lo-ammi. This means 'Not my people.' For Israel is not mine, and I am not her God." (Hosea 1:6-9)*

RELATED VERSES: *Genesis 30:8; 1 Samuel 25:25; Isaiah 8:1-4; Matthew 1:21*

Q: DOES SATAN KNOW ABOUT THE BIBLE?

94

A: Satan knows all about the Bible. He even knows what it says. But Satan certainly doesn't follow what the Bible teaches. In fact, he does everything he can to stop people from obeying God's Word. Just because someone knows the truth doesn't mean that he or she will do it. Satan is a liar, the father of lies. He has lied and twisted the truth so much that he has fooled himself into thinking that what the Bible predicts won't happen. Satan thinks that he can beat God and escape his punishment. But the Bible tells the truth. Eventually God will totally wipe out Satan and his demons.

KEY VERSES: *Are there still some among you who hold that "only believing" is enough? Is believing in one God enough? Well, remember that the demons believe this. And they shake with fear! Fool! Don't you know that "believing" is useless unless you do what God wants? Faith that does not result in good deeds is not real faith. (James 2:19-20)*

RELATED VERSES: *Matthew 4:6; John 5:39-40*

RELATED QUESTION: *If Satan knows the Bible, why doesn't he believe it?*

THE
CHURCH

Q: WHY DO WE GO TO CHURCH IF GOD IS EVERYWHERE?

95

A: In the Bible, God tells us to join other Christians and worship him. We should spend time alone, praying and reading his Word. But it is also very important to get together with others who follow Christ. We can encourage and strengthen each other. We can pray for each other. We can learn from each other. We can sing and praise God together. We can serve and help each other. All of this can happen in church. Church is also a place where Christians of all ages and types can come together—babies, grandparents, children, poor, wealthy, brown, black, white, American, Asian, African, weak, strong, and so on. Something very special happens when God's family gets together.

KEY VERSE: *Let us not neglect our church meetings, as some people do. Encourage and warn each other. Do this especially now that his day of coming is near. (Hebrews 10:25)*

RELATED VERSES: *1 Chronicles 16:29; Acts 2:42-47; 1 Corinthians 11:23-25; 12:12-31*

RELATED QUESTION: *Why do we have to go to church?*

NOTE TO PARENTS: *Many children find church boring. That's because the service is usually geared for adults. But it also may be because children have not been taught how to worship. Take time to explain the purpose behind the church programs (like Sunday school, church dinners, the worship service, and so forth) and each part of the worship service (for example, songs, Communion, offering, and so forth). Help your child understand what he or she should be doing and why.*

Q: WHY DO WE WORSHIP GOD?

96

A: Worship means praising and thanking God for who he is and for what he has done. People worship in many different ways. Worship can involve group singing, group reading, special music, giving money, prayer, Communion, Bible reading, teaching, preaching, and other activities. God has given us everything good that we have. He loves us and wants the very best for us. Shouldn't we spend time with him and tell him how grateful we are? We play with our friends because we enjoy them. We worship God because we enjoy him.

KEY VERSES: *Jesus replied, "Something new is coming. Then we will not worry about whether to worship here or in Jerusalem. For it's not where we worship that counts, but how we worship. We must worship in spirit and in truth. For God is Spirit, and we must worship him in truth." (John 4:21-24)*

RELATED VERSES: *Exodus 20:3; 1 Chronicles 16:29*

RELATED QUESTION: *Why do we have to do something that isn't fun?*

Q: HOW COME MY FRIENDS GO TO A DIFFERENT CHURCH?

97

A: In most homes, parents decide where children will go to church if they go. Some people go to a certain church because they grew up in that church. Even after moving across town, they drive there every Sunday to be with friends and family. Some people choose a church because they enjoy a certain style of worship. There are many reasons for choosing a church. But some churches really aren't true churches according to the Bible's teachings. Real churches honor Jesus, study God's Word, tell people to give their lives to Christ, and emphasize obeying God. Churches are groups of God's people, meeting together to worship, fellowship, serve, and learn.

KEY VERSES: *If someone says, "I love God," but hates his brother, he is a liar. He doesn't love his brother who is right there in front of him. So how can he love God whom he has never seen? And God said that one must love not only God but his brother too. (1 John 4:20-21)*

RELATED VERSES: *Acts 2:1; Hebrews 10:24-25*

RELATED QUESTION: *Why are there different types of churches?*

Q: WHAT PART OF THE BODY OF CHRIST AM I?

DRESS REHERSAL

98

A: The Bible uses word pictures to explain how Christians relate to each other. We are a "family," with brothers and sisters in Christ. We are a "building," with Christ as the cornerstone. We are a "body," with each person serving as a special part. God talks about us being a body to show how Christians should treat each other and work together. God has given each Christian special gifts. That means each of us has talents and abilities that can be used to help other believers. Not everybody has the same gifts. And, like the parts of a body, we need each other. All of our gifts are important.

KEY VERSES: *There are many parts to our bodies. It is the same with Christ's body. We are all parts of his body. It takes every one of us to make it complete. We each have different work to do. We belong to each other, and each needs all the others. (Romans 12:4-5)*

RELATED VERSES: *Romans 12:6-8; 1 Corinthians 12:1-30*

NOTE TO PARENTS: *This is a question usually asked only by older children (junior high or older) who have heard teaching on the body of Christ. Encourage them to get involved with a gift or talent they have.*

Q: WHY DO PEOPLE GET BAPTIZED?

BAPTISMAL
TANK

99

A: People get baptized because Jesus was baptized, and they want to follow his example. They also get baptized because Jesus told his followers to go into all the world, telling people about him and baptizing them. Some Christians believe that babies from Christian families should be baptized to show that they belong to Christ. Some Christians think that only believers in Christ should be baptized, to show that Jesus is their Savior. Either way, baptism is a very important event in a Christian's life.

KEY VERSE: *And Peter replied, "Each one of you must turn from sin and come back to God. Then you must be baptized in the name of Jesus Christ. For through him, you will find forgiveness for your sins. Then you also shall be given this gift, the Holy Spirit." (Acts 2:38)*

RELATED VERSES: *Matthew 3:13-17; 28:19*

Q: WHAT HAPPENS TO PEOPLE WHO DON'T GO TO CHURCH?

SUNDAY
SERVICE
10:00 A.M.

100

A: Going to church doesn't get a person into heaven. And not going to church doesn't send a person to hell. A person becomes a Christian by faith—believing in Christ—not by doing good things. Most Christians go to church because of what happens there. At church you can meet other Christians. You can find help for your problems and encouragement. You can learn from God's Word and help others. And you can experience wonderful worship, singing, and praying that glorifies God. People who don't go to church miss all that. They miss a very special meeting with God.

KEY VERSES: *Then what can we brag about doing to earn our salvation? Nothing at all! Why? Because we were not forgiven because of our good deeds. Instead, we were forgiven because of what Christ has done and our faith in him. So we are saved by faith in Christ, not by the good things we do. (Romans 3:27-28)*

RELATED VERSES: *Ephesians 2:8-9; Hebrews 10:24-25*

RELATED QUESTION: *Does God send people to hell if they don't go to church?*

Q: WHEN IS JESUS COMING BACK?

A: Before Jesus left the earth many years ago, he promised to return some day. And after Jesus went up into the clouds, angels said he would come back eventually. No one knows exactly when that will happen. It could be any day now. For Christians, this is a wonderful event to look forward to. Christ's return will be the beginning of the end for Satan and all evil in the world. Won't it be great to see Jesus in person! Although no one knows when Christ will return, he told us to be ready. This means living the way he would want us to, using our time wisely, and telling others about God's Good News.

KEY VERSES: *[Jesus is speaking] "But no one knows the date and hour when the end will be. Not even the angels know this. No, not even God's Son knows this. Only the Father knows. . . . So be ready at all times. For you don't know what day your Lord is coming." (Matthew 24:36, 42)*

RELATED VERSES: *Matthew 24:27, 42-51; John 14:3; 1 Corinthians 1:7; Colossians 3:4; 1 Thessalonians 5:2-3; 2 Thessalonians 2:1-3; 2 Peter 3:12-13; Revelation 22:20*

RELATED QUESTION: *When can we really see Jesus?*

Part II

Questions Children
Ask about Heaven and Angels

General Editor
Daryl J. Lucas

Written by
David R. Veerman, M.Div.
James C. Galvin, Ed.D.
James C. Wilhoit, Ph.D.
Bruce B. Barton, D.Min.
Richard Osborne

CONTENTS

THE END OF THE WORLD

MISTER AND MISCELLANEOUS

INTRODUCTION

Children have lots of questions about heaven and angels. We know. We collected hundreds before they turned off the spigot.

Some of their questions are easy to answer, such as "Can you fall out of heaven?" But many others strike at the heart of our ignorance. Haven't you ever heard a child ask, "Why can't I see Jesus now?" Hmm . . .

Easy responses to tough questions are "I don't know," "Just because," and "Because I said so!" Those may be responses, but they're not answers. And they certainly don't help the child sort truth from error.

That's why we wrote this book: to help you answer children's tough questions about heaven and angels.

The questions come entirely from real children (with a little editing for clarity). We surveyed children ages three to twelve and collected their responses, then sorted them (the questions, not the children) until we identified the 104 most common and important ones. If you are a parent or if you work with children very often, you will surely hear questions like these—if you haven't already!

The answers, however, come entirely from Scripture. For every question, we looked in the Bible for the most relevant passages, then summarized their application to that question. Take time to study the Scriptures listed because the Bible is our final authority. God's Word alone reveals what we know about heaven and angels.

As you answer children's questions, keep the following points in mind.

- "Silly" questions are serious questions. Always take children's questions seriously. Don't laugh at them. Some questions may sound silly to you, but they're not silly to your child. Be careful not to ridicule your child's imaginative ideas.

- Some questions hide fears or insecurities. For example, when a little girl asks, "Are all people nice in heaven?" (question 42), she's asking about her own safety, not just heaven. She knows what bullies are like, and she's afraid of them. She wants assurance that in heaven no one will be mean to her or push her around. Go ahead and answer the question behind the question—assure your child that there are no bullies in heaven. If you suspect that there may be a hidden question but don't know what it is, a great way to get at it is to ask, "Why do you ask?" or "Why do you want to know?"

- The best answers come from Scripture. The Bible doesn't answer every curiosity we have, but it is our only authoritative source for information on heaven and angels. The best thing you can do to prepare to answer questions like these is to study the Scriptures yourself.

- The best answers avoid theological jargon. Use normal words. Children think in literal terms, so abstract concepts don't mean a thing to them. As much as possible, talk about *things, events,* and *objects* they can imagine. Describe a smell. Mention a thing. Talk about an action, such as running. Give them something to look at in their minds. If they can see it, they will understand it.

- Some questions have no answer. Be careful not to make up an answer when you don't have one and when the Bible is silent. If you don't have an answer, say so. Or suggest that you look for the answer together. If you get in the habit of inventing answers, your children will later lump faith with stories and superstitions they've discovered were false. Emphasize the truths of Scripture that you *do* know.

• Some kids just want to keep asking. Be ready for follow-up questions, and be willing to keep talking. Your answer may lead to more questions. That's the mark of a good answer—it makes your child think.

We wrote this book to help you answer kids' questions about heaven and angels. We sincerely hope and pray it does that.

—Dave Veerman, Jim Galvin, Jim Wilhoit, Bruce Barton, Daryl Lucas, Rick Osborne, Lil Crump

ANGELS

Q: WHERE DID ANGELS COME FROM?

102

A: God created everything, and that includes angels. The Bible doesn't say, "God created angels," nor does it mention when God created angels. But we know he did because the Bible explains that God created everything that exists. The Bible never says that God created dogs, for example, but we know that he did because he created all things. We also don't know if God created all the angels at once or if he creates them as he needs them. Angels take orders from God and serve him. They aren't equal with God and don't have the same powers as God. Remember, God didn't discover angels—he created them.

KEY VERSES: *Praise [God], all his angels, all the armies of heaven. . . . Let everything he has made give praise to him. For he gave the command, and they came into being. (Psalm 148:2, 5)*

RELATED VERSES: *Nehemiah 9:6; Colossians 1:15-16*

RELATED QUESTIONS: *On which of the seven days did God create the angels? How did God discover angels? Are angels like people except that they live in heaven? Do angels have mothers? How did God get the idea to make angels? How were angels made? Did God make angels?*

NOTE TO PARENTS: *Try to avoid using the word* angel *when it is inaccurate, such as calling your child a "little angel" or saying that a person who died has become an angel. These innocent explanations can easily confuse children.*

Q: DO ANGELS HAVE NAMES?

103

A: The Bible mentions two angels by name—Gabriel and Michael. We don't know if all angels have names, but they probably do since angels are personal beings, like people. Even though they don't have bodies, they have identities, just like people. But they're not human beings. They are God's servants. He created them to do his work. Remember, the only place that we can learn for sure about angels is in the Bible, God's Word.

KEY VERSE: *"Don't even ask my name," the Angel replied. "For it is a secret." (Judges 13:18)*

RELATED VERSES: *Daniel 8:16; 10:13; Luke 1:19, 26; Jude 1:9; Revelation 12:7*

RELATED QUESTIONS: *How does God remember all the angels? How come God only named two angels in the whole Bible? Was the angel's name beyond understanding because it was too hard to say (Judges 13:18)?*

Q: DO ANGELS HAVE HEARTS?

To my Guardian angel
my very special
valentine!
xoxoxo
from Jason
+ Max

A:

If you're asking whether angels have feelings, the answer is yes. Angels have feelings just as people do and just as God does. Many Bible passages tell of angels *rejoicing* whenever someone first believes in Jesus. Others tell of angels singing songs of gladness and praise to God.

Angels can also think. The Bible says they can tell the difference between good and evil. Satan and his demons used to be good angels, but they chose to do evil. (More on that in question 24.) The Bible also says that angels care about us and that they helped Jesus.

But angels don't have real hearts because they don't have physical bodies.

KEY VERSE: *There is joy among the angels of God when one sinner repents. (Luke 15:10)*

RELATED VERSES: *2 Samuel 14:17, 20; Psalm 34:7; 91:11; Luke 2:13-14; Hebrews 12:22-23; Revelation 5:11-12*

RELATED QUESTION: *Do angels get angry?*

Q: DO ANGELS GROW UP?

105

A: You may have seen paintings or cartoons of "baby angels," but those are not true pictures of angels. Angels don't have physical bodies, so they are never born, they never grow up, and they never die. They don't need to eat or drink, and they don't outgrow their clothes. But they can learn—they can get more knowledge than they started with. The Bible says that angels learn from watching people (they "grow in knowledge"). Angels are learning more and more of God's wisdom all the time.

KEY VERSE: *[God] wanted to show all the rulers in Heaven how perfectly wise he is. They will see the Jews and Gentiles joined together in his Church. (Ephesians 3:10)*

RELATED VERSES: *Matthew 22:30; 1 Peter 1:12*

RELATED QUESTIONS: *Do angels live like we do today? Does God have to teach his angels to do things? Do angels have ages? Can angels have children? Do angels take care of themselves? Does God tell them stories?*

NOTE TO PARENTS: *We associate growth with change. That is, we talk about people "growing" spiritually, mentally, and in other areas to describe the changes we see happening in them. When children ask, "Do angels grow up?" however, they are usually referring to physical growth—aging and getting bigger, stronger, faster, etc.*

Q: ARE ANGELS BOYS OR GIRLS?

106

A: *People* are either male or female (boys or girls) because of their bodies—the way they are physically. But angels don't have physical bodies, so they are neither boys nor girls. (Jesus explained that angels don't get married.) The angels Michael and Gabriel have male names, but that doesn't mean that they are men. When angels visited people in human form (when Gabriel visited Mary, for example), usually it was as a man.

KEY VERSE: *For in the resurrection there is no marriage. Everyone is like the angels in Heaven. (Matthew 22:30)*

RELATED VERSES: *Mark 12:25; 16:5; Hebrews 1:14; 13:2*

RELATED QUESTIONS: *Are there girl angels, or are they all boys? When I die, will I become an angel?*

Q: DO ANGELS GET TIRED?

The sign in the image reads: "JASON'S GUARDIAN ANGEL'S RECOOPERATION STATION"

107

A: Angels never get tired, not even a little bit, and they never sleep. They don't need sleep like you do. Good angels are incredibly powerful and always ready to do what God tells them to do. Angels can open locked doors, roll away huge stones, and even wipe out whole armies. That's because they are God's servants, and God gives them the power they need to carry out his work. Angels are not all-powerful, though. The book of Daniel tells of a time when Satan stopped an angel for a little while, until the archangel Michael came to help him. But angels never get tired, weak, or sick. And someday they will fight in the final battle against Satan and his demons—and *win*.

KEY VERSE: *Suddenly there was a great earthquake. For an Angel of the Lord came down from Heaven. He rolled aside the stone and sat on it. (Matthew 28:2)*

RELATED VERSES: *Psalm 103:20; Daniel 9:21-23; 10:13; Acts 5:19; 2 Peter 2:11; Revelation 12:7-8*

RELATED QUESTIONS: *How can angels be so strong that they were able to keep the lions' mouths from closing? Do angels help out other angels? Just how strong are angels? Do angels sleep?*

Q: DO ALL ANGELS HAVE BLONDE HAIR?

108

A: Actually, the Bible never says that angels have hair. Whenever the Bible describes them as appearing as people, it doesn't mention what color their hair is. Remember, angels don't have bodies like humans do. You may have seen paintings of angels with blonde hair, or you may have seen cartoons that show them that way, but we don't know exactly what angels looked like when they appeared to people. They *can* appear with blonde hair, but they don't have to. The Bible does say, however, that they often appeared as shining, radiant, or glorious beings. Maybe that's where people got the idea that they must have blonde hair. But then it would be just as likely that they had *red* hair. Right?

———

KEY VERSE: *The angels are your messengers. They are your servants of fire! (Psalm 104:4)*

RELATED VERSES: *Luke 2:9-10; John 20:12; Acts 12:7; 2 Thessalonians 1:7; Hebrews 1:7*

RELATED QUESTIONS: *What do angels look like? Are angels as bright as the sun? Are some angels black?*

Q: DO ANGELS HAVE HALOS?

HEE HEE
HA HA

109

A: Many drawings of angels or of people in the Bible show them with little rings of light over their heads that look a lot like round fluorescent light-bulbs. Those are called halos. But there is no evidence in the Bible that anyone, human or angel, ever had a halo. Real angels don't look anything like those pictures. Some passages in the Bible describe angels as very bright beings. Their clothes or their faces shine with bright light, glow like hot metal, or gleam like the sun. This is because angels reflect the glory of God. (When Moses met with God on Mount Sinai, his face took on a glow because he had been with God.) Angels don't *have* to come shining brightly, but many of them do. Halos have become a popular way of showing that angels give off God's glory or brightness, but they don't give a very good picture of the glory and power that angels actually have.

KEY VERSES: *As I [Daniel] stood there, I looked up. And suddenly there stood before me a person dressed in linen clothes. He had a belt of purest gold around his waist. And his skin was glowing and lustrous! From his face came blinding flashes like lightning. And his eyes were pools of fire. His arms and feet shone like polished brass. His voice was like the roaring of a great crowd of people. (Daniel 10:5-6)*

RELATED VERSES: *Matthew 28:2-3; Luke 2:9; 24:4; 2 Thessalonians 1:7*

RELATED QUESTIONS: *Are angels' clothes shiny? Do angels wear clothes?*

Q: WHY CAN'T I SEE ANGELS?

110

A: The Bible tells of angels appearing to people. Why don't they appear to us today? It may seem unfair or strange that you can't see angels, but angels are spirits. They don't have bodies as we do. Angels appear with physical bodies only when God sends them to speak to people. The times when angels have appeared to people (at least the ones we know about for sure) have been quite rare—only during the Exodus, the time of the judges, the time of Elijah, the time of Jesus' birth, and the time of the forming of the early church. In other words, God doesn't show off his angels. He saves angelic appearances for times when people really need to see them. Angels can do their work without being seen.

KEY VERSE: *An Angel of the Lord came and spoke to Philip. The Angel said, "Go over to the road that runs from Jerusalem through the Gaza Desert. Be there around noon." (Acts 8:26)*

RELATED VERSES: *Psalm 34:7; Acts 10:22*

RELATED QUESTIONS: *Will God let us see an angel in these days? How come God wants it so you can't see the angels? How come angels disappear?*

NOTE TO PARENTS: *The real question here may be, If angels are real, why can't I see them? Explain to your child that there are a lot of things that are real that they can't see, such as electricity, oxygen, etc.*

Q: ARE THERE PEOPLE INSIDE OF ANGELS?

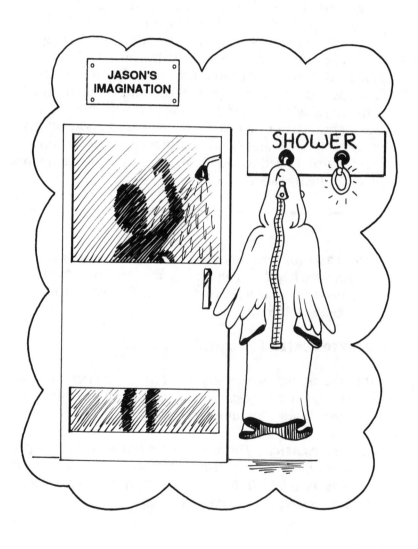

111

A: People and angels are two different kinds of beings altogether. There aren't any people inside angels, nor do people become angels when they die. In cartoons you may see people die and become angels, but that's not what really happens. People have souls. Our souls live forever as spiritual beings. In fact, here's a cool secret: When we get to heaven, we will get to rule the angels!

KEY VERSE: *Don't you know that we will judge the angels in Heaven? (1 Corinthians 6:3)*

RELATED VERSES: *Mark 12:25; Hebrews 2:5-8*

RELATED QUESTIONS: *How does a person become an angel? Were angels people before they died? Will we become angels when we get into heaven?*

Q: HOW MANY ANGELS ARE IN HEAVEN?

112

A:

There's a huge number. We don't know how many angels are in heaven because the Bible doesn't give an exact number. But there are thousands and thousands—as many as God needs. Some people who have seen these large crowds of angels are Elisha and his servant, the shepherds at Christ's birth, and the apostle John.

KEY VERSE: *Then I [John] heard the singing of many angels. They were surrounding the throne and the Living Beings and the Elders. (Revelation 5:11)*

RELATED VERSES: *2 Kings 6:16-17; Luke 2:13; Hebrews 12:22; Revelation 7:9-11*

RELATED QUESTIONS: *How many angels are there? Does God have a sidekick angel? Does God have grandchildren in heaven?*

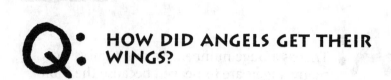

Q: HOW DID ANGELS GET THEIR WINGS?

JASON'S IMAGINATION

113

A: Artists often paint angels as having wings, and people have written stories that describe angels as having wings or earning their wings. But the Bible doesn't say that all angels have wings. It does say that angels can fly and that, at times, they appear with wings. But angels don't need wings to fly, like birds or butterflies do. God made sure that they can get where they need to be when they need to be there.

KEY VERSE: *As I [Daniel] prayed, Gabriel flew swiftly to me. He is the angel I had seen in the earlier vision. (Daniel 9:21)*

RELATED VERSES: *Isaiah 6:1-2; Ezekiel 1:6-9, 23-24*

RELATED QUESTIONS: *Why do angels fly? Do angels look the same as the ones we make in the snow? Do angels really look like they do in pictures? Do all angels have wings? How come in pictures angels have wings? Do angels have wings, or do they just look like men in pajamas?*

Q: CAN ANGELS DIE?

114

A: If angels had bodies like people do, they would die, just like people do. But angels don't have bodies. They're spiritual beings, which means that they have no flesh or blood. Angels are spirits, invisible to us but still very real. Angels aren't born, either—they're created. Because angels don't have bodies, they can't grow old and die. But at the final judgment after the world ends, God will destroy Satan and the bad angels (see Revelation 20:11-14).

KEY VERSE: *[People] will never die again. In these ways they are like angels and are sons of God. For they are raised up in new life from the dead. (Luke 20:36)*

RELATED QUESTIONS: *If angels fight, can they get hurt? Do angels take care of themselves?*

WHAT ANGELS DO

Q: DO ANGELS GO TO WORK?

115

A: The word *angel* means "messenger." Angels don't have jobs where they work for pay, the way people do. Instead, they serve God. Angels do nothing but what God wants them to do all the time, without ever getting tired or grumpy. They're happy to do it. They do a lot of work, but they don't "go to work" like your mom or dad does.

KEY VERSE: *The angels are spirits who serve God. They are messengers sent to care for those who will receive [Christ's] salvation. (Hebrews 1:14)*

RELATED VERSES: *Luke 4:10; 16:22; Revelation 4:8; 7:15*

RELATED QUESTIONS: *What does my angel do? Can angels build things? Why does God use angels—why doesn't he do everything?*

Q: DO ANGELS WATCH TELEVISION?

116

A: Angels spend all their time doing what God wants them to do and praising him. They don't take time to relax or do things "just for fun." Keep in mind that angels don't need to relax, because they don't get tired. And they enjoy their service to God so much that stopping to do something else wouldn't be "fun" for them anyway. Why would angels want to watch the stuff on TV when they can see the stars up close, fly through the universe doing errands for God, and watch God doing miracles in people's lives? Angels have much better things to do than watch TV—they help us!

KEY VERSE: *These Living Beings . . . didn't rest day or night. They said, "Holy, holy, holy, Lord God Almighty! He was, and is, and is coming." (Revelation 4:8)*

RELATED VERSES: *Hebrews 1:14; Revelation 7:11-12*

RELATED QUESTIONS: *What do angels do all day long when they are not protecting people from getting kidnapped? Can angels get bored?*

Q: DOES EACH ANGEL BELONG TO A PERSON?

117

A:

The Bible says that angels help people, but it doesn't say each angel watches over a certain person like a bodyguard. You may have heard people say that God assigns an angel to watch over each person, but we don't know whether that's true. We only know that God gives angels the job of helping and protecting us. We don't know how they divide that job.

KEY VERSE: *Be careful that you don't look down upon a single one of these children. For I [Jesus] tell you that in Heaven their angels can speak directly to my Father. (Matthew 18:10)*

RELATED VERSES: *Psalm 34:7; 91:11; Ezekiel 28:14; Hebrews 1:14*

RELATED QUESTIONS: *Does every person have a guardian angel? Do I have a guardian angel?*

NOTE TO PARENTS: *There is a Jewish tradition that angels look like the person to whom they are assigned.*

Q: ARE THERE ANGELS IN THIS ROOM WITH US?

118

A: Angels aren't everywhere, so we shouldn't expect them to be with us at every moment, the way God is. But angels *may* be in the room with you right now. Angels *can* be with us without our knowing about it. In the Bible story about Balaam (Numbers 22:21-41), Balaam didn't know there was an angel with him until God allowed him to see the angel. Angels are invisible spirits, so we never know exactly where they are.

KEY VERSE: *Don't forget to be kind to strangers. Some who have done this have served angels without knowing it! (Hebrews 13:2)*

RELATED VERSES: *Numbers 22:22-35; 2 Kings 6:16-17; Hebrews 1:14*

RELATED QUESTION: *Why are angels kept in heaven?*

Q: DO ANGELS STAY IN THE CAR OR FLY BESIDE?

119

A: God watches over us, using angels as his servants. If God wants an angel to be with you in the car, that is where the angel will be. If God wants the angel to be outside the car and moving along at sixty-five miles per hour, that's where the angel will be. Angels go wherever God tells them to go.

KEY VERSE: *Shall I look to the mountains for help? No! My help comes from the Lord. (Psalm 121:1-2)*

RELATED VERSE: *Matthew 28:20*

RELATED QUESTIONS: *Do angels protect us all the time? If angels are always around us, how come some people die?*

Q: DO ANGELS SIN?

120

A: We don't know if angels can sin anymore.
Human beings sin because they have a desire
to sin. That is because after Adam and Eve disobeyed
God in the Garden of Eden, every person ever born has
been born a sinner. Angels are not like human beings,
and they don't have a desire to sin. So it is not natural
for angels to disobey God.

The Bible hints that they may be able to do wrong.
Satan was once an angel who was thrown out of heaven
because he wanted to take God's place. And other angels
sinned then by following Satan. But can other angels sin
now? We don't know. We know only that heaven cannot
have any sin in it; if it did, it would not be perfect.

KEY VERSE: *God cannot even trust his own messengers. Even
angels make mistakes! (Job 4:18)*

RELATED VERSES: *Job 15:15; 2 Peter 2:4; Jude 1:6*

RELATED QUESTIONS: *Does God like it when people say to
you, "Oh, you are a little angel"? Do angels do what they
are supposed to do by themselves, or does God have to tell
them what to do? How do angels know to obey God? If
angels were bad once, can they still be bad?*

Q: CAN AN ANGEL BE YOUR FRIEND AND TELL YOU THAT HE IS YOUR ANGEL?

OK THE RULES ARE...
NO ONE CAN GO IN SWIMMING
WITHOUT A 'BUDDY' TO WATCH
OUT FOR YOU!

121

A: In the Bible, we learn that God wants to be good friends with people. He doesn't give that job to angels. God called Abraham his friend. God spoke to Moses in the way that a man would speak to a friend. That's what he wants with us, too. God's angels do his work, but they don't try to become friends with us because the one looking for our friendship is God. If God has given you an angel, you won't see that angel or talk to him.

KEY VERSE: *I [Jesus] no longer call you slaves. For a master doesn't confide in his slaves. Now you are my friends. This is proved by the fact that I have told you all that the Father told me. (John 15:15)*

RELATED VERSE: *Exodus 33:11*

RELATED QUESTIONS: *Can I talk to angels? Can you play with angels? Can you have a relationship with an angel?*

Q: DO ANGELS JUST APPEAR FOR AN INSTANT ONE MINUTE AND THEN DISAPPEAR?

122

A: Angels are not ghosts, gods, or superheroes. They serve God and always follow his directions, so they go wherever he says and appear however he tells them to. They appear to us the way they need to appear to do God's work. In the Bible we sometimes read of angels coming and going quickly, but they never did it to show off. In fact, usually no one saw them appear or disappear.

KEY VERSE: *Suddenly, the angel was joined by a great crowd of others. All the armies of Heaven were there! They were praising God. (Luke 2:13)*

RELATED VERSES: *Luke 2:8-15*

NOTE TO PARENTS: *Some children may ask this question because they think they may have seen an angel, and they want to know if it is possible. Others may ask this because of the way angels are pictured in movies and television shows. Emphasize the fact that the only reliable source for our information about angels is the Bible.*

Q: CAN AN ANGEL BE A PERSON TO US LIKE A REAL PERSON?

123

A: Sometimes angels have made themselves look like humans and have appeared to people. That's how they appeared to Abraham one day. Abraham was sitting outside his tent when three men walked up and greeted him. As far as he knew, they were men, perhaps travelers looking for a place to stay. But in fact, they were angels. That's why the Bible urges us to be kind and neighborly to visitors. You never know when a visitor might be an angel. It is possible that you have met an angel and did not know it. But don't go looking for angels. Angels almost always stay invisible.

KEY VERSE: *Don't forget to be kind to strangers. Some who have done this have served angels without knowing it! (Hebrews 13:2)*

RELATED VERSES: *Genesis 18:1-2*

RELATED QUESTIONS: *Can we talk to our angels, to the ones who protect us? Does everyone have their own personal angel?*

BAD
ANGELS

Q: ARE DEMONS RED WITH HORNS AND LONG TAILS?

124

A: Sometimes cartoons and Halloween costumes show the devil and demons as red creatures with horns and long tails. But that idea of what Satan looks like came out of someone's imagination, not from the Bible. The devil is a bad angel, and angels don't have physical bodies, so no one knows what Satan looks like. Like other angels, the devil can take different forms if he wants to. But he's not a red-clothed lizard with a pitchfork. He's a real being, living in the spiritual realm.

Satan is God's enemy, but Satan is not as powerful as God. When Satan was created, he was good. But he later rebelled against God and was kicked out of heaven. Jesus called him "a liar and the father of lies." The Bible says he is an "angel of light." So we see that Satan can be very tricky—he tries to make bad look good. His main way of doing this is to lie to us and accuse us, not scare us with the way he looks.

KEY VERSE: *I remind you of the angels who were pure and holy. But they turned to a life of sin. Now God has them chained up in prisons of darkness. They are waiting for the Judgment Day. (Jude 1:6)*

RELATED VERSE: *1 Peter 5:8*

RELATED QUESTIONS: *Who is the devil? Can demons look like angels like Satan can? Did God actually kick the devil out of heaven?*

NOTE TO PARENTS: *Kids have the idea that the devil is God's equal, like a villain in a superhero cartoon. But the devil is no match for God. God is infinite and all-powerful, while Satan is a created being with limited power.*

BAD ANGELS

Q: WHY DID GOD MAKE SATAN IF GOD KNEW SATAN WOULD MAKE SIN?

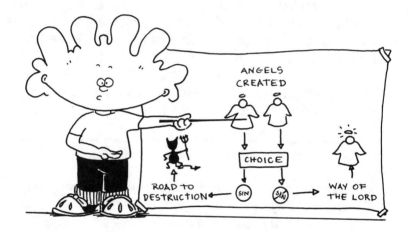

125

A: God created all people and all angels with the ability to choose to obey him. God knew that some would choose to obey and some would choose to disobey. Still he created them because he knew it was a good thing to do. God makes everything good, and that includes the people and angels, who had the choice of whether or not to serve God. Also, Satan did not invent sin, but he tries to get people to choose it. God has allowed Satan to have freedom now, but in the end God will defeat Satan and punish him.

───────────────

KEY VERSE: *I [Jesus] saw Satan falling from Heaven like a flash of light! (Luke 10:18)*

RELATED VERSES: *Revelation 20:7-10*

RELATED QUESTIONS: *If heaven was so perfect and Satan lived there before he sinned, why did he sin? Why didn't God stop Adam from eating the apple off the tree? Why did God make a bad tree in the Garden with Adam and Eve?*

Q: DOES THE DEVIL HAVE POWER LIKE GOD DOES?

126

A: The devil has great powers, but he is not even close to being as powerful as God. Satan can perform fake miracles, lie, accuse, twist the truth, tempt, and trick people into doing what is wrong. But he also has many limits: He cannot be everywhere at the same time; he cannot create anything; he is not all-powerful; he cannot read your mind; and he has no power over Jesus.

KEY VERSES: *Dear friends, don't be afraid of these who want to murder you. They can only kill the body. They have no power over your souls. But I'll tell you whom to fear! Fear God who has the power to kill you and then put you into hell. (Luke 12:4-5)*

RELATED VERSES: *Job 1:6-12; 2:1-7; John 14:30*

RELATED QUESTIONS: *Is Satan as powerful as God? Does Satan ever get hurt? What is Satan's kingdom made up of? Why was Satan a snake when he tempted Eve?*

NOTE TO PARENTS: *You can assure your child that the devil has no power over Jesus (John 14:30). That's just one reason it's so great to be Jesus' friend.*

Q: WHAT MEAN THINGS DOES SATAN DO TO PEOPLE?

127

A: Satan does *not* get to do whatever he wants to do to people. The main thing he does is get us to hurt ourselves and others. Lots of people think that Satan only tempts people to do bad stuff. He does tempt us, but the worst thing he does is lie to us. Satan hates God and does not want us to believe what God says. He wants us to sin. He wants us to believe what is false. He wants us to believe that we are no good. Satan lies to us about our worth and about what really matters so we'll hurt ourselves. The way to see Satan's lies is to know the truth that's in the Bible, God's Word.

KEY VERSE: *Watch out for attacks from Satan, your great enemy. He prowls around like a hungry, roaring lion. He is always looking for someone to tear apart. (1 Peter 5:8)*

RELATED VERSES: *Genesis 3:1; Job 1:6-12; 2:1-7; Matthew 4:1; John 8:44; 14:30; 1 John 3:8; Revelation 12:9-10*

RELATED QUESTIONS: *Will I ever get a demon? Can people be demon possessed? Do demons live in some people's hearts?*

NOTE TO PARENTS: *Some children have heard of demon possession and wonder if it can happen to them. They may ask a question like this as a veiled way of asking the more frightening one. But the devil has no power over Jesus. If we have Jesus in our hearts, Satan won't be able to do whatever he wants to with us or make us do anything we don't want to do.*

BAD ANGELS

Q: HOW COME THE DEVIL WANTS US TO BE BAD?

Satan's Destruction Program

TEMPTATION

SIN

ROAD TO DESTRUCTION

ETERNAL SUFFERING

128

A: Satan's main purpose is to make us part of his kingdom, not just to make us bad. The devil would be quite happy if you lived a good life but never did anything for Jesus. He doesn't want you to serve God. He wants to hurt your faith in God, to make you doubt God's love and goodness. One of the ways he does that is to tempt you to do bad things. If Satan had his way, Christians would just sit around, doing nothing good and telling no one about Jesus.

KEY VERSE: *Then [false teachers] will come to their senses and escape from Satan's trap. He uses it to catch them whenever he likes. Then they can begin doing the will of God. (2 Timothy 2:26)*

RELATED VERSES: *John 17:15; 1 Peter 5:8-9*

RELATED QUESTIONS: *Why is the devil after us? Why was Satan so wicked? Why did Satan become so mean? Why is Satan so jealous? Why did Lucifer become bad?*

NOTE TO PARENTS: *Satan's main job is to lie to people, to get non-Christians to stay away from God, and to prevent Christians from serving God. He plants doubts and tries to convince us that we're not God's children.*

Q: ARE SATAN AND JESUS STILL AT WAR?

129

A: Jesus and Satan are definitely enemies at war, but Jesus will win. (By the way, when Jesus says to love your enemies, he's not talking about loving the devil. He's talking about loving people.) The devil will do everything in his power to try to stop people from believing in Jesus and living for Jesus. But we don't have to be afraid of Satan because God protects his people against Satan's power. Jesus never loses.

KEY VERSES: *Put on all of God's armor. Then you will be safe from Satan's attacks. We are not fighting against people made of flesh and blood. We are fighting against persons without bodies. They are the evil rulers of the unseen world. They are the satanic beings and evil princes of darkness who rule this world. They are the huge numbers of wicked spirits in the spirit world. (Ephesians 6:11-12)*

RELATED VERSES: *Hebrews 2:14; 1 John 2:14; Revelation 2:11; 12:7*

RELATED QUESTIONS: *Does Satan ever talk to God? Does God know the devil? Why does Satan want to be stronger than God? What does Jesus do all day? Does Jesus have a job in heaven? Does Jesus sleep?*

Q: WILL GOD FORGIVE SATAN?

130

A: God will never forgive Satan because Satan hates God and doesn't want to be forgiven. He doesn't want to have a relationship with God or to live in God's presence. He wants to take God's place. But God has already told us what will happen to Satan—he will be punished by being thrown in the lake of fire (hell), where he will suffer forever for his rebellion.

KEY VERSE: *Then the devil who tricked them will be thrown into the Lake of Fire. It is burning with sulfur where the Creature and False Prophet are. They will be tormented day and night forever and ever. (Revelation 20:10)*

RELATED VERSES: *Revelation 20:7-10*

RELATED QUESTIONS: *Can Satan turn back and become good? Why doesn't God kill Satan? If Satan knows that he isn't going to win against God, why doesn't he just become good again? Why did Satan start doing wicked things if he was an angel? Does God still love Satan, even when he does bad things to people?*

NOTE TO PARENTS: *Many people confuse niceness with God's love. They think that a loving God should be nice to everyone, even Satan. But a loving God does not love evil.*

Q: CAN AN EVIL SPIRIT STOP YOU FROM GOING TO HEAVEN?

131

A: If a person has given his or her life to Christ, nothing can stop that person from going to heaven. The only thing the devil can do is invent lies that sound like truth and then hope people believe them. Satan can't send you to hell or keep you from going to heaven, no matter what he does.

KEY VERSES: *I am sure that nothing can ever separate us from [Christ's] love. Death can't, and life can't. The angels won't. All the powers of hell can't keep God's love away. . . . It doesn't matter if we are high above the sky, or deep in the ocean. Nothing can carry us away from God's love that is in our Lord Jesus Christ. (Romans 8:38-39)*

RELATED VERSES: *John 14:30; Philippians 1:6*

RELATED QUESTIONS: *Who goes to hell? Are there kids in hell? Can Christians go to hell? How do evil spirits come into you?*

Q: WHAT IS HELL LIKE?

HELL = Satan + fire + bugs + Snakes + whips + scorpions

132

A: According to the Bible, hell is very dark and very painful. It is a place of eternal suffering and separation from God. It is a place of grim loneliness. The worst thing about hell is that it is separate from God and from all that is good. There is no love, joy, fun, laughter, or celebration in hell. Some people make jokes about hell and say that they want to go there to be with their friends. But no one will have any friends in hell. No one should want to go there.

KEY VERSE: *But [the rich man's] soul went into hell. There, in torment, he saw Lazarus far away with Abraham. (Luke 16:23)*

RELATED VERSES: *Matthew 5:22; 8:12; 25:41, 46; 2 Thessalonians 1:9; 2 Peter 2:4; Revelation 9:1-2, 11; 14:10-11; 20:10*

RELATED QUESTIONS: *Why is there hell? Where is hell? Is there fire in hell? Why is hell dark if they have fires? Is it hot in hell? Was there a fire when the devil went down to hell?*

NOTE TO PARENTS: *Be very serious when you explain hell to your children. At the same time, however, tell them about heaven, a place of eternal love, joy, fun, laughter, and celebration. And assure them that they can go to heaven if they trust in Jesus.*

ANGELS
IN THE
BIBLE

Q: WHY DID AN ANGEL COME TO MARY?

133

A: An angel came to Mary to tell her God's message—God wanted Mary to know that she would be the mother of Jesus, God's Son. When Mary heard the news, she was frightened, but she was also very happy. More than anything, she wanted to obey God. And she felt very honored to be Jesus' mother.

KEY VERSE: *God sent the angel Gabriel to Nazareth. (Luke 1:26)*

RELATED VERSES: *Luke 1:26-38*

RELATED QUESTIONS: *What was the name of the angel who came to Mary? What angel came to tell the shepherds about Jesus' birth?*

NOTE TO PARENTS: *This is a good time to let your children know that God is able to show them his plan for their lives. God's plan probably won't be announced by an angel, but God will tell it to them when they seek him.*

Q: WHY WAS THERE AN ANGEL AND A FIERY SWORD GUARDING THE ENTRANCE TO THE GARDEN OF EDEN?

134

A: An angel stood at the entrance to the Garden of Eden to keep Adam and Eve from going back in. God had sent them out of the Garden because they had sinned. Because they disobeyed God, they would never be allowed to live in Eden again.

KEY VERSE: *God expelled [Adam]. And God placed mighty angels at the east of the Garden of Eden. They stood with a flaming sword to guard the entrance to the Tree of Life. (Genesis 3:24)*

RELATED VERSES: *Numbers 22:31; 1 Chronicles 21:27-30; Luke 4:10*

RELATED QUESTIONS: *How did Satan disguise himself as a snake? Did the serpent bite? When you're in heaven, can you still see the angel that is guarding the entrance to Eden? Did Adam and Eve go to heaven when they died?*

Q: WHO WAS THE ANGEL OF THE LORD?

135

A: The Bible mentions the angel of the Lord many times. In the desert, when Moses saw the bush that was burning but wasn't burning up, it was the angel of the Lord who spoke to him out of it. Who was this who spoke? Some people think it was a special appearance of God and not actually an angel. But usually the phrase "angel of the Lord" is just a good way to describe an angel. It probably does not refer to one specific angel.

KEY VERSE: *The Angel of the Lord came to [Gideon]. He said, "Mighty soldier, the Lord is with you!" (Judges 6:12)*

RELATED VERSES: *Exodus 3:2; Numbers 22:22; 2 Samuel 24:16; 1 Chronicles 21:16*

RELATED QUESTION: *Why do people call an angel "angel of the Lord"?*

NOTE TO PARENTS: *It is important to help your child focus on God, not on angels. The message sender and the message are most important, not the messengers.*

Q: WHY DO SOME ANGELS LOOK LIKE REAL PEOPLE?

136

A: The word *angel* means "messenger," and God sometimes sends these messengers to take messages to people. The Bible describes them as bringing these messages while in the form of human beings. God can send angels to encourage a person, comfort someone, or merely to deliver news. If angels always appeared as blazing towers of fire, they would scare people away. Sometimes God wants angels to frighten people. But at other times he wants his messengers to hide their true identity as angels for a while; then they appear as people.

KEY VERSE: *All at once [Abraham] saw three men coming toward him. He jumped up and ran to meet them and welcomed them. (Genesis 18:2)*

RELATED VERSES: *Genesis 19:1; Judges 6:11-12; 13:15-18; Daniel 9:21; Acts 12:7; Hebrews 1:14*

RELATED QUESTION: *Can angels be here with us?*

Q: WHY DO SOME ANGELS HAVE FOUR FACES?

137

A: When the Bible describes angels as having four faces, it is not giving us a picture of what angels actually look like (like a photograph). Remember, angels don't have physical bodies, so they don't have faces the way people do. When a prophet saw an angel with four faces, God was telling him that angels have many abilities—that angels show us several things about God, that they can see in any direction, and that they can serve God in any way needed at any time.

KEY VERSE: *Each of the four Guardian Angels had four faces. The first was that of an ox. The second was a man's face. The third was a lion's face. And the fourth was an eagle's face. (Ezekiel 10:14)*

RELATED VERSES: *Ezekiel 10:1-22*

Q: WHY DIDN'T AN ANGEL TAKE JESUS OFF THE CROSS?

138

A: It was God's will for Jesus to die on the cross. Jesus could have called on thousands of angels to rescue him, but he did not do that because he was dying for us, taking the punishment for our sins. If angels had stepped in and rescued Jesus, he would not have died, and then we would not be forgiven. Jesus' disciple Peter tried to stop Jesus from being arrested, but Jesus told him not to do that because it was God's plan for him to die.

Just before Jesus died, he cried out, "My God, my God, why have you forsaken me?" meaning that God had left him totally alone. No one was there to help him or comfort him, not even the angels. This was part of his suffering for our sins.

KEY VERSES: *Don't you know that I [Jesus] could call on my Father? He could send thousands of angels to keep us safe! And he could send them right away! But if I did this, how would the Scriptures be fulfilled? For they foretold what is happening now. (Matthew 26:53-54)*

RELATED VERSES: *Matthew 26:51-54; Mark 8:31; 15:34-37*

RELATED QUESTIONS: *Where were the angels when Jesus died? Why didn't an angel take Jesus' crown off of him? Why did an angel come to the tomb after Jesus had left?*

Q: **WHICH ANGEL IS BEST AFTER GOD AND THEN JESUS?**

139

A: The Bible uses the word *archangel* to describe one type of angel that seems to be more important than regular angels. Only Michael is said to be an archangel, but we don't know if he is the only one. The Bible also refers to princes among the angels. That seems to suggest that some angels are more powerful than others. Angels are not equal to Jesus, though. They aren't gods, nor are they God's buddies. Angels are created beings who obey and worship God.

KEY VERSE: *For 21 days the Evil Spirit who rules the kingdom of Persia blocked my [the angel's] way. Then Michael, one of the top officers of the heavenly army, came to help me. So I was able to get past these spirit rulers of Persia. (Daniel 10:13)*

RELATED VERSES: *Daniel 10:21; 1 Thessalonians 4:16; Hebrews 1:3-13; 2:5-8; Jude 1:9*

RELATED QUESTION: *Does God have a bodyguard?*

Q: WHY ARE SOME PEOPLE SCARED OF ANGELS?

140

A: In the Bible, we read that some people became frightened when angels appeared to them. They were scared because they were amazed at the power and glory of the angels. God is great and holy and awesome, and sometimes angels appear with a lot of light and noise. That can be quite scary. Also, remember that most people have never seen an angel. So when one appears, it is quite normal to be surprised and fearful. Many times when angels appeared, they had to tell the people they visited not to be afraid. God sends angels to us to help us, so we don't need to be afraid of them.

KEY VERSE: *Then the Angel touched the meat and bread with his staff. Fire flamed up from the rock and burned them up! And suddenly the Angel was gone! (Judges 6:21)*

RELATED VERSES: *1 Chronicles 21:30; Matthew 28:2-4; Luke 1:13, 28-30; 2:9-10; Revelation 22:8-9*

HEAVEN

WHY DID GOD MAKE HEAVEN?

141

A: God has only one use for heaven, and that is to share it with us. God is everywhere. When we talk about heaven, we are really talking about where God lives. We think of heaven as a place because that's how we describe going to be with God. But remember, God isn't just in one place—he's everywhere!

In the Bible, the word *heaven* can refer to several places: (1) the home or place of God; (2) the new Jerusalem; or (3) "the heavens," or sky. Just before Jesus left the earth, he said he would go and prepare a place for us, a place where we can live with him. Someday he will come back and set it all up for us—he will destroy this world and create a new one. That new world will be for all those who love him. That's the heaven that God will make for all believers to live in forever.

KEY VERSES: *There are many homes in my Father's house. I am going to prepare a place for you. I will come again and take you to me. Then you will be with me where I am about to go. If this weren't so, I would tell you plainly. (John 14:2-3)*

RELATED VERSES: *Hebrews 9:24; Revelation 21:3*

RELATED QUESTIONS: *What is heaven? What is heaven like? Why did God come to the earth? Is hell near heaven?*

NOTE TO PARENTS: *Heaven is one of the Christian's great hopes. It is God's guarantee that the evil, injustice, and cruelty of life here on earth will end and be put right. People without hope in Christ can feel overwhelmed by fear of the future, but Christians need not be afraid. Share this hope with your child.*

HEAVEN

Q: IS JESUS THE ONLY WAY TO HEAVEN?

142

A: Yes, Jesus is the only way to heaven. He said, "No one can get to the Father except through me." Just as the only right answer to 2 + 2 is 4, Jesus is the only answer to our need for forgiveness. He is the only one who has the right to take away our sins, since he died for us. He is the only one who has the power to take them away, since he is God. And he is the only one who can be perfectly fair to every single person, from babies never born to the most wicked person who ever lived, since he is just and merciful. Since Jesus has offered a clear way to heaven, why would anyone look for any other way?

KEY VERSE: *Jesus said, "I am the Way, the Truth, and the Life. No one can get to the Father except through me." (John 14:6)*

RELATED VERSES: *John 6:68; Revelation 22:17*

RELATED QUESTIONS: *Why is heaven the only way? If you believe in God but you never asked Jesus as your Lord and Savior, can you still go to heaven? If babies die before they are born, do they go to heaven?*

NOTE TO PARENTS: *A question like this usually means that other children were discussing their beliefs with your child. Take this time to reassure your child that belief in Christ is the only way to heaven, and take some time to pray with your child for his or her friends.*

Q: ARE ALL PEOPLE NICE IN HEAVEN?

HEAVEN

143

A: All the people in heaven are nice because everyone there loves God and loves one another. No one will hurt anyone or be mean to anyone in heaven. There will be no crying or pain. There will be no pushing or shoving or name-calling in heaven. The Bible says that in heaven we will know God like he knows us. When we know and understand God and his love, we won't want to hurt anyone ever again.

KEY VERSE: *Don't you know that those doing such [evil] things can't share in God's Kingdom? (1 Corinthians 6:9)*

RELATED VERSES: *Revelation 21:4, 8; 22:14-15*

RELATED QUESTIONS: *Will bullies call me names in heaven? What if someone bad tricks Jesus and sneaks into heaven and hits people?*

NOTE TO PARENTS: *Be careful not to give the impression that being nice gets you into heaven. While all people of God should be kind, not all kind people are people of God. Also, the question behind the question here may involve fear of others—the child wants assurance that in heaven no one will hurt him or her. You can assure your child that there are no bullies in heaven. Heaven is the safest, most wonderful place ever made.*

Q: CAN YOU FALL OUT OF HEAVEN?

144

A: People cannot fall out of heaven any more than they can fall out of their own front yard. You may have seen pictures or cartoons that show heaven as a place up in the sky or in the clouds. We don't know where heaven is; we only know that God and Jesus are there. Someday God will make a new earth and a new city called the new Jerusalem, where all his people will live forever. That place will be perfect for us—no dangerous streets, no diseases to catch, nothing to worry about at all. In heaven, you will never hear anyone say, "Be careful!" because you won't have any dangers to be careful about.

KEY VERSE: *I heard a loud shout from the throne. It was saying, "Look, the home of God is now among men. He will live with them and they will be his people. Yes, God himself will be among them." (Revelation 21:3)*

RELATED VERSES: *Romans 8:39; Revelation 22:14*

RELATED QUESTIONS: *Are there police in heaven? Will there be any doors in heaven? Does heaven move?*

NOTE TO PARENTS: *This question comes up when children confuse heaven with a physical location, usually one that is up in the sky. They are not able to imagine a spiritual—as opposed to physical—reality, so they can't imagine heaven not being a place. They naturally think of heaven as being up because that's where we put it in our descriptions of it.*

Q: IS HEAVEN ALL MADE UP OF CLOUDS?

JASON'S IMAGINATION

145

A: Sometimes cartoons and movies show funny pictures of angels standing in clouds. But heaven is not made up of clouds. The Bible does say that clouds surround God's throne, that Jesus was caught up in the clouds, and that when Jesus returns he will come in the clouds. But those are word pictures. They don't mean that heaven is made up of rain clouds. Heaven is God's presence. It's a spiritual place. It's a world invisible to us now but very real just the same.

KEY VERSE: *Then the scene changed. I saw a white cloud. Someone was sitting on it, and he looked like Jesus. He was called "The Son of Man." He had a crown of gold on his head and a sickle in his hand. (Revelation 14:14)*

RELATED VERSES: *Psalm 97:2; Luke 21:27; 1 Thessalonians 4:17*

RELATED QUESTIONS: *Is there going to be summer and fall in heaven? Will there be any winter? Will our house be warm? Does it rain in heaven? Can you walk on clouds in heaven? Are there bathrooms in heaven? Is there water in heaven?*

NOTE TO PARENTS: *Children pick up a lot of wrong ideas about heaven from cartoons and other popular tales. If you're not sure how to explain what's wrong with a false idea, it's better to say "I don't know how to explain it" than to fall back on a popular fantasy. Sit down with them and read Revelation 21–22 together so they can see what the Bible says about heaven and the new Jerusalem.*

Q: WHY IS HEAVEN SO SHINY?

146

A: Heaven shines with the brightness of the glory of God. God is perfect, holy, 100 percent good. Because of that, God shines with light. Many descriptions of heaven mention light and gold because of God's glory.

KEY VERSE: *Great bursts of light flashed forth from him. It was like light from a glittering diamond or from a shining ruby. There was a rainbow glowing like an emerald around his throne. (Revelation 4:3)*

RELATED VERSES: *Revelation 4:1-6; 21:18-21, 23; 22:5*

RELATED QUESTIONS: *Will there be night in heaven? Why does God stay up all night? What does my mansion in heaven look like?*

Q: ARE THE STREETS IN HEAVEN REAL GOLD OR JUST PAINTED WITH GOLD?

147

A: All of heaven is real—none of it is fake. When we get there, it will be the most real, beautiful place we have ever seen. Will even the gold be real? The Bible says that the streets will be paved with gold. This may just be a way of saying that it's a great place to be, like saying "It must be a million degrees out here" to describe a really hot day. Or it may refer to real gold streets running through town. It's hard to know *exactly* what heaven will be like because we really can't understand it now.

Imagine a frog trying to explain life on land to a tadpole. All the descriptions would sound bad—you can't swim, there's no water, etc. The frog can't really tell the tadpole what life on land is like. Only when the tadpole becomes a frog can the tadpole understand. Only when we get to heaven will we know what it will be like. But one thing is for sure: Nothing will be fake!

KEY VERSE: *The 12 gates were made of pearls. Each gate was made from a single pearl! And the main street was pure, clear gold, like glass. (Revelation 21:21)*

RELATED VERSES: *Revelation 21:1–22:21*

RELATED QUESTIONS: *What will God's house be made of? What will God's house look like in heaven? Is heaven more beautiful than the most beautiful place on earth? What is heaven made of? How does God make things out of gold? Does God use glue to make gold stick to the new Jerusalem? Are the gates in heaven made out of gold?*

Q: DOES GOD HAVE ANGELS WATCHING OVER HEAVEN SO DEMONS CAN'T GET IN?

148

A: God will let no evil at all into heaven—no sin, no hurting, no demons. Life in heaven will be *safe*. In fact, heaven is the safest place anywhere—perfectly safe all the time. No one in heaven is afraid of anything, and no one there ever gets hurt.

KEY VERSE: *[God] will swallow up death forever. The Lord God will wipe away all tears. He will take away all insults and mockery against his land and people forever. The Lord has spoken! He will surely do it! (Isaiah 25:8)*

RELATED VERSES: *Revelation 7:17; 22:3-5*

RELATED QUESTIONS: *Is heaven a safe place? Will I be safe in heaven? Does God keep bad stuff out of heaven? Can the devil still hurt you when you're in heaven? Will snakes be there? Will we be able to see Satan in heaven?*

NOTE TO PARENTS: *Every child craves safety and fears danger. A safe place is a happy place, and conversely, a dangerous place isn't. In order to be happy, a child needs to feel safe. A question like this one, therefore, applies a child's test of happiness to heaven: If it isn't safe, then it can't be happy. You can reassure your child that no place is safer than heaven.*

Q: WHERE DID GOD LIVE BEFORE HEAVEN WAS MADE?

149

A: God has always lived in heaven because heaven is the place where God is. God has made a place for us where he is—so that is heaven for us. Wherever God is, there is heaven.

KEY VERSE: *Our Father in Heaven, we honor your holy name. (Matthew 6:9)*

RELATED VERSES: *Deuteronomy 26:15; 1 Kings 8:30, 39, 43, 49*

RELATED QUESTIONS: *Where does God live? How does God get down here (to live in us)—does he fly? How can God be in more than one place at one time? How long did it take to make heaven?*

NOTE TO PARENTS: *Sometimes a child's question comes from a faulty assumption about God. You can use questions like this to explain how God is different from us.*

Q: DOES JESUS LIVE WITH GOD IN HEAVEN, OR DOES HE LIVE BY HIMSELF?

150

A: When Jesus left the earth, he went to heaven to live with God the Father. That's where he is right now. He sits at the Father's right hand, the place of highest honor. The Bible says he talks to God about us (1 John 2:1).

KEY VERSE: *Now I am leaving the world, and leaving them behind. And I am coming to you. Holy Father, keep them in your own care. Keep all those you have given me. May they be united just as we are. (John 17:11)*

RELATED VERSES: *John 17:5; Acts 7:55-56; Romans 8:34; Colossians 3:1; Hebrews 10:12*

RELATED QUESTIONS: *Will Jesus do miracles in heaven? Is Jesus happy in heaven? When God is in heaven, is he always thinking of people down here on earth? Does God take care of his angels the way he takes care of his people? Is God like the president of the United States in heaven?*

Q: WHY DOESN'T GOD TAKE US TO HEAVEN AS SOON AS WE GET SAVED?

SEE, THIS IS WHAT JESUS DID FOR US.

JESUS

BIBLE STORIES FOR KIDS

151

A: God doesn't take his people to heaven right away because he wants them to grow in their faith. He also wants them to tell others about Christ, to help others, and to make the world better. God has work for his people to do.

KEY VERSES: *So now go and make disciples in all the nations. Baptize them into the name of the Father, the Son, and the Holy Spirit. Then teach these new disciples to obey all the commands I have given you. (Matthew 28:19-20)*

RELATED VERSES: *John 9:4; 2 Peter 3:9*

Q: WHAT IF I DON'T WANT TO LEAVE MY FRIENDS AND FAMILY TO GO TO HEAVEN?

152

A: It's OK to not want to go to heaven right now. God has given you a place to enjoy right here and now—your home and your family and friends. You don't have to go to heaven right away.

But heaven will be a happy place, not a lonely or a sad place. Once you're in heaven you won't feel afraid of it—you will be glad that you are there. And if your family and friends know Jesus, too, you all will be in heaven together. You will be together with your family again.

KEY VERSE: *Be sure of this thing! I am with you always, even to the end of the world. (Matthew 28:20)*

RELATED VERSES: *Revelation 21:3-5*

RELATED QUESTIONS: *Will I be able to play with my friends up in heaven? How can you get out of heaven? What will my friend do when he goes to heaven? Do they have sports in heaven?*

NOTE TO PARENTS: *Don't be appalled if your child says he or she is afraid of heaven or doesn't want to go. Some kids fear going to heaven because it seems faraway and mysterious. All they can imagine is being taken away from their families and going to a cold and impersonal place where they don't know anyone. Assure your child that heaven is a warm and happy place.*

Q: HOW LONG DOES IT TAKE TO GET TO HEAVEN FROM HERE?

153

A: It happens in an instant. It's like opening your eyes—you're suddenly there. That's because heaven isn't a faraway place but is the place where God is. He just takes you there. The Bible says that when Jesus comes back, he will change us "in the twinkling of an eye."

KEY VERSE: *It will all happen in a moment, in the twinkling of an eye. (1 Corinthians 15:52)*

RELATED VERSES: *2 Corinthians 5:6-8; Philippians 1:21-23; 1 Thessalonians 4:13-17*

RELATED QUESTIONS: *Is heaven far out in space? Where is heaven? Can birds just fly into heaven anytime they want to? If we went high enough into the sky, would we find heaven? Why can't we go to heaven and just see it and then come back? When you die, are you just dead for a few seconds and then you're in heaven?*

Q: DOES GOD PUT DOWN A LADDER TO BRING US TO HEAVEN?

JASON'S IMAGINATION

154

A: God takes us to heaven as soon as we die—immediately. God doesn't need a ladder or an airplane or anything else; we will just be there with him. The Bible says that Jesus is preparing a place for us. Through faith in him, we can have forgiveness of sins. Then, when it comes time for God to take us to heaven, he will do it—he will take us to live with him in his home forever.

KEY VERSE: *The Lord himself will come down from Heaven. This will happen with a mighty shout. There will be the voice of the archangel and a trumpet of God. The believers who are dead will be the first to rise to meet the Lord. (1 Thessalonians 4:16)*

RELATED VERSES: *Luke 16:22-31; John 14:6*

RELATED QUESTIONS: *Do angels take people's souls up to heaven? Will Jesus help me fly up? How will Jesus get me there? How do we get to heaven? How does God get people to heaven? Does God put down a ladder so that when people die they just climb up it into heaven? Do angels carry me to heaven? Does God take us to heaven? Does Jesus come for you with his body?*

NOTE TO PARENTS: *This question can mean two things: (1) What method does God use to transport us to heaven? and (2) How can a person be forgiven and go to heaven? Make sure you know which question your child means. In Jesus' story about the rich man and Lazarus (Luke 16:22), he mentioned that the angels carried Lazarus to heaven. Angels may be involved in the process.*

WHEN
PEOPLE
DIE

Q: WHY DO PEOPLE DIE?

155

A: People die because of sin. When God created the first human beings, they weren't supposed to die. They would never grow old or wear out. But then they disobeyed God, and sin and death entered the world. From that point on, every person born has been born a sinner into a sinful world. With sin came death, and so plants, animals, and people started to die. *Every* person has to die. But people can live eternally, in heaven with God, if they trust in Christ and ask God to forgive their sins. In heaven we aren't broken anymore. There is no sickness or pain or dying there.

KEY VERSES: *You may eat any fruit in the garden except fruit from the Tree of Conscience. You must not eat from that tree. For its fruit will open your eyes. It will make you aware of right and wrong, good and bad. If you eat its fruit, you will be doomed to die. (Genesis 2:16-17)*

RELATED VERSES: *Romans 6:23; 1 Corinthians 15:22; Hebrews 9:27; James 1:15*

RELATED QUESTIONS: *What is death? Why do I have to die? Why do some people die when they're young and not just when they're old? If God wants everyone to live, why do babies die? Do you grow older when you go to heaven?*

NOTE TO PARENTS: *This question often comes up when a relative or a pet dies. It is a good question and an important one for you to answer because it creates a "teachable moment." Answering it will probably lead to several more questions about salvation, eternal life, and heaven, so be prepared!*

Q: DOES YOUR BODY STAY IN THE GRAVE WHEN YOU GO TO HEAVEN?

156

A: The body you have here on earth is a physical, imperfect, short-term holding place for your soul. It's not made to last. When it's dead, it will decay. The real you is your soul, not your body. But in heaven you will be given a new body, a body that will last forever. This is known as the resurrection. The physical body will die, but the spiritual body will last forever. What happens to your body on earth or in the grave will not affect your eternal life in any way.

KEY VERSE: *For you [God] will not leave me among the dead. You will not let your loved one rot in the grave. (Psalm 16:10)*

RELATED VERSES: *Psalm 49:15; 1 Corinthians 15:35, 42-44*

RELATED QUESTIONS: *Will we be able to breathe in heaven? Does your spirit have clothes on when it leaves your body, or is it naked? What does it feel like when your spirit leaves your body? When you die are you automatically in heaven?*

Q: WILL I GO TO HEAVEN WHEN I DIE?

157

A: Every person who trusts in Jesus gets to go to heaven. If you have asked Jesus to take away your sins, then you will go to heaven, too. That's God's promise. And nothing can take away God's promise of heaven. When you die as a Christian, you go straight to live with God—you don't need to be afraid of dying.

KEY VERSE: *It is God's will that I should not lose even one of all those he has given me. It is his will that I should raise them to eternal life at the Last Day. (John 6:39)*

RELATED VERSES: *Isaiah 12:2; Romans 8:38-39; Hebrews 2:14; 6:11; 10:19-22; 2 Peter 1:10-11; 1 John 5:13*

RELATED QUESTIONS: *What if I die when I'm six or seven or eight? When will I die? When will we be dead? When I die, will I go straight to heaven?*

NOTE TO PARENTS: *Many children have a profound fear of death. They may have nightmares about it. But they may also hesitate to talk about it with you, so you may not hear them ask about it. Reassure them: Jesus defeated death. He made it possible for us to live forever in heaven. We don't need to fear death.*

Q: IS THERE ANY OTHER PLACE YOU CAN GO TO BESIDES HEAVEN OR HELL WHEN YOU DIE?

158

A: You may have heard people talk about purgatory, limbo, or some other in-between place where people go after they die. But the Bible does not teach anything about a place like that. The Bible does teach, however, that death is the final cutoff point. People do not have a second chance after they die. There is no opportunity after death to undo the bad things a person did while alive. The Bible also makes it very clear that Christians immediately go to be with God after they die.

KEY VERSE: *Jesus replied, "Today you will be with me in Paradise. This is a solemn promise." (Luke 23:43)*

RELATED VERSES: *Psalm 86:13; Proverbs 1:12; Luke 23:40-43; Hebrews 9:27*

RELATED QUESTION: *Does your soul stay in your body until you are buried or just until you die?*

Q: CAN GOD TAKE YOU TO HEAVEN IF YOU'RE NOT DEAD YET?

159

A: God can do anything. He can take a person to heaven anytime he likes, even if that person has not died. And in fact, the Bible tells about two people who had that privilege: Enoch and Elijah. God took them directly to heaven before they died. The Bible also tells us that someday Jesus will come back and take all his people to heaven, even those who have not died yet.

KEY VERSE: *When [Enoch] was 365, he disappeared. God took him away! (Genesis 5:24)*

RELATED VERSES: *2 Kings 2:11-12; 1 Corinthians 15:51; 1 Thessalonians 4:15-17*

RELATED QUESTIONS: *Why did Elijah get taken into heaven by a whirlwind when he hadn't died yet? Will we go to heaven in a fiery chariot?*

Q: WHY ARE CEMETERIES SO CREEPY?

160

A: Death is a scary thing because it is final. After a person dies, that person does not come back to earth ever again. It's not like going on a trip and then coming back. It's like going on a trip and *never* coming back.

Death also scares us because it can happen so suddenly. One second the person is here, awake and talking. Then he or she is dead, unable to talk or live with us ever again.

That's why cemeteries are so creepy. No one wants to die, and cemeteries are where dead bodies are buried. Also, television and movies show cemeteries as places where ghosts and other spooky things hang out. Because most people fear death, a cemetery can be a scary place. But Christians don't have to be afraid of death because they know that they will go to heaven when they die and that scary things are just made up by people who make movies and TV shows.

KEY VERSES: *Even now, just as in the past, I hope that I will be an honor to Christ. This is true whether I live or die. For to me, living is Christ, and dying—well, that's better yet! (Philippians 1:20-21)*

RELATED VERSES: *Proverbs 10:24; Luke 8:49-56; Romans 8:38-39; 1 Corinthians 3:22*

RELATED QUESTIONS: *Why is everybody buried together in a cemetery instead of by themselves? How can they make room in the cemetery for everyone who is dead?*

NOTE TO PARENTS: *Help your children develop a healthy attitude about death. Say positive things as you pass a cemetery; don't jokingly say things that foster a fear of death.*

161

A: We don't like to think about this fact, but it is true—eventually every person has to die. Sometimes people die when they are young, through accidents, diseases, or other tragedies. But even the healthiest person will die someday. As we get older, our bodies get weaker and weaker and then finally wear out.

No one wants a grandfather or grandmother to die, but that's part of God's plan right now: We get old and our bodies die. Certainly it is better to be with God in heaven than to be on earth. If our grandparents believe in Jesus, then someday we will see them again.

KEY VERSE: *[God's] loved ones are very special to him. He does not lightly let them die. (Psalm 116:15)*

RELATED VERSES: *Proverbs 16:31; 20:29*

RELATED QUESTIONS: *When I go up to heaven will I see my grandma? Will God let me visit Grandpa in heaven? If a whole family dies on earth, like in a fire, will they be together in a house in heaven?*

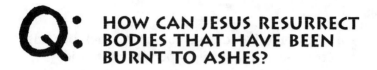

Q: HOW CAN JESUS RESURRECT BODIES THAT HAVE BEEN BURNT TO ASHES?

162

A: God will have no trouble finding everyone's molecules. He created people in the first place, so why wouldn't he be able to put them back together? It doesn't matter what happens to a person's body—God can put anyone back together. Whether the person's body was burned, separated for organ donations, or decayed in the ground, God will make it new and immortal. The earth and sea will give up their dead, and God will resurrect us despite the fact that we "returned to dust."

KEY VERSES: *When Jesus comes back, God will bring back with him all the dead Christians. . . . The believers who are dead will be the first to rise to meet the Lord. Then we who are alive and remain on the earth will be caught up with them. We will go to the clouds to meet the Lord in the air. We will stay with him forever. (1 Thessalonians 4:14, 16-17)*

RELATED VERSES: *Psalm 90:3; Ecclesiastes 3:20; Revelation 20:12-13*

RELATED QUESTIONS: *How can Jesus resurrect your body if it's turned to compost? If people have been dead for a long time, do they turn to compost? If someone hurts you really bad, like a bad person cuts off your head, and God really loves you, will he give you a new body? Isn't it gross to have worms chewing your body after you're dead?*

Q: WHY DO PEOPLE BELIEVE IN REINCARNATION?

A: Reincarnation is the belief that people come back to life after they die. They never really die once and for all but keep coming back as something else or as someone else. This belief says that people come back to earth as different creatures after they die.

Some people believe in reincarnation because their religion, such as Hinduism or Buddhism, teaches it. Some believe in reincarnation because they want to believe that they will get a second chance on earth to be better people. But the Bible does not teach reincarnation. The Bible teaches that we have one life and then we face judgment.

KEY VERSE: *It is planned that men die only once. And after that comes judgment. (Hebrews 9:27)*

RELATED VERSES: *Luke 16:19-31*

RELATED QUESTIONS: *Does* born again *mean reincarnation? Is reincarnation replanting carnations? If you die, can you come back as a different person? What does the Bible say about reincarnation?*

NOTE TO PARENTS: *Some children misinterpret the term* born again *to mean reincarnation. You can explain that being born again means to be born into God's family, not to come back as a different person later. Being born again happens when we trust in Jesus Christ as Savior. It's not reincarnation.*

Q: WHAT'S A CASKET?

DISPLAY CASKETS

HEAVEN'S DELIVERY BOX

HEAVEN'S DELIVERY BOX

164

A: A casket is a metal or wooden box in which a dead body is placed. Usually a casket is buried in the ground in a cemetery. Putting a body in a casket is a very old custom and is a way of showing respect for the dead person. Also, it is part of the custom of mourning the person's death.

KEY VERSE: *It will be an honor to have you [Abraham] choose the finest of our tombs, so that you can bury [Sarah] there. (Genesis 23:6)*

RELATED VERSES: *Genesis 50:26; Amos 2:1; Mark 15:46; Romans 12:15*

RELATED QUESTIONS: *How can people be cremated? How can adults be cremated when they're so big?*

Q: WHY DO PEOPLE CRY AT FUNERALS?

165

A: People cry at funerals because they are very sad. They miss the person who has died. Even when people know that their family member or friend is now in heaven with Jesus, they cry because they miss their loved one. The purpose of funerals is to say good-bye to the dead person, to show respect for the person and his or her family, to cry and be sad, and to remember what the person meant to everyone.

KEY VERSES: *Tears came to Jesus' eyes. "They were close friends," the Jewish leaders said. "See how much he loved him." (John 11:35-36)*

RELATED VERSES: *Mark 5:38-39; Luke 7:11-15; Romans 12:15*

RELATED QUESTION: *Why do we have funerals?*

Q: WHY DO THEY PUT STONES ON PEOPLE'S GRAVES?

166

A: A gravestone or metal plate on a grave marks the place where the person's body is buried. After a person has died, friends and family will sometimes go to the cemetery, put flowers on the grave, and think about that person. The stone helps them find the grave. They can go there and remember the person instead of forgetting. Just think what it would be like if a family member was buried and no one marked where the grave was.

KEY VERSE: *The Lord buried [Moses] in a valley near Beth-peor in Moab. But no one knows the exact place. (Deuteronomy 34:6)*

RELATED VERSE: *Acts 13:36*

RELATED QUESTIONS: *Why do people talk to dead people at their graves? Why do people visit people's graves if their spirits have already gone to heaven?*

Q: WHY DO WE GIVE FLOWERS TO PEOPLE AFTER THEY HAVE DIED?

167

A: Many people bring flowers to funerals, wakes, and gravesides. It looks as though they are giving something to someone who can't enjoy the gift. Why would they do that? It is to show respect and to show that they miss the person. It's like saying, "I wish you were still here. I love you. I miss you." Also, flowers remind us of life. Most important, people give flowers to honor the person and the family of the person who has died. Flowers on a casket or on a grave say, "This person was important to me."

KEY VERSE: *When others are happy, be happy with them. If they are sad, share their sadness. (Romans 12:15)*

RELATED VERSES: *Isaiah 40:6; Amos 2:1; 1 Peter 1:24; 2:17*

LIVING
IN
HEAVEN

Q: WILL I BE ABLE TO PLAY GAMES IN HEAVEN?

168

A: Heaven will be more exciting than you could possibly imagine. Will that mean playing lots of games? Probably not—you can get bored with games, and life in heaven will *never* be boring. You will never get tired of what you're doing there. The Bible says that you will always be happy in heaven. If you think games are fun, you should see what's coming next—it will be *much* better than playing games all the time.

It's OK if you don't understand this. Trying to understand life in heaven is like trying to understand how fun an amusement park will be before you get there. How can you really know what to expect? You can't. All you can do is hear the descriptions ("It's great! It's wonderful! You can ride on the SuperCollosalMachine!"). Until you go, you won't *really* be able to get excited about it. But once you're there, *wow!*

KEY VERSE: *We can see and understand only a little about God now. It is like we were looking at his reflection in a poor mirror. Someday we are going to see him face to face. Now all that I know is hazy and blurred. But then I will see everything clearly. (1 Corinthians 13:12)*

RELATED VERSES: *1 Corinthians 13:11-12; Revelation 4:8-11; 7:15-17; 22:3*

RELATED QUESTIONS: *Will there be lots and lots of toys in heaven? Will I still get to drive a car when I'm in heaven, or can you take a bus somewhere?*

NOTE TO PARENTS: *The tadpole analogy (see the next question) is useful for questions about boredom in heaven.*

Q: IN HEAVEN, WE DON'T JUST SING AND WORSHIP ALL DAY, DO WE?

169

A: In heaven, we will be happy all the time. Heaven will be a place made just for us. We read in the Bible about angels singing and praising God day and night, and we can't imagine doing that all the time. But remember that they are singing because they are *glad*. They aren't bored, tired, or old. They are expressing happiness and joy. God is the happiest person in the universe, and living in heaven means being there with him doing the same thing. Life with God is happy, joyful, and cool.

Imagine that you're a tadpole. All your life you've lived only in the water. You know that someday you'll become a frog and you'll get to live on land. But until you become a frog, you will have no idea what life on land is like. And if anyone tries to explain it to you, it won't sound very appealing because there's no water and you can't swim. That's the way it is with heaven. Until we get to heaven, it will be hard for us to understand what's so great about it. But once we're there, we'll be perfect and we'll have new bodies, and that will make all the difference.

KEY VERSE: *Now I can sing glad praises to the Lord. I can sing instead of lying in silence in the grave. (Psalm 30:12)*

RELATED VERSES: *Psalm 61:8; 89:1; Isaiah 35:10; 51:11; 1 Corinthians 2:9; 13:12; Revelation 4:8-11; 7:15-17*

RELATED QUESTIONS: *Won't heaven be boring? Will I be bored in heaven?*

NOTE TO PARENTS: *Children can understand singing for joy by thinking of songs they sing when they're happy or celebrating. What they feel when singing those songs is like what they will feel in heaven—only better!*

LIVING IN HEAVEN

Q: WHAT WILL I DO UP THERE WITH NO FRIENDS?

170

A: If your friends believe in Jesus, they will be in heaven with you, and you will have a *great* time together. Jesus is preparing a place for us; he won't keep us apart from each other. And we'll make new friends in heaven, too. If you aren't sure whether your friends will go to heaven, tell them about Jesus. If they put their faith in Christ, too, you will all be there together.

You don't have to worry—heaven *won't* be boring. Remember, God created butterflies, sunsets, electrical storms, mountains, the Grand Canyon, and all of nature. He will give us so much fun, beauty, and joy in heaven that we can hardly imagine it now.

KEY VERSES: *There are many homes in my Father's house. I am going to prepare a place for you. I will come again and take you to me. Then you will be with me where I am about to go. (John 14:2-3)*

RELATED VERSES: *1 Thessalonians 4:13-17*

RELATED QUESTIONS: *Who can I play with when I die? Will I be able to play with my friends up in heaven? Will I remember my family and friends in heaven? Will there be any stuffed animals? Is there going to be any paint in God's world? What happens when we go to heaven?*

Q: WILL I STILL HAVE FEELINGS IN HEAVEN?

JASON'S IMAGINATION

171

A: Yes! People in heaven have lots of feelings—all good ones. People in heaven are filled with joy! You will be busy smiling, whistling, and singing for joy. When you are not doing that, you will be kicking your heels and jumping. Occasional high fives will interrupt the joviality. The timing will be perfect, and you'll love it. You will be happy because you will be with God and because all sin, death, and sadness will be gone forever. And think of the joy when you see your family and friends. Heaven will be a place of great joy and gladness—great feelings all around.

KEY VERSE: *You will give me back my life. You will give me great joy in your presence. (Acts 2:28)*

RELATED VERSES: *Jeremiah 31:13; Matthew 25:34; John 16:20-22*

Q: CAN WE STILL HAVE BIRTHDAYS IN HEAVEN?

172

A: The great thing about birthdays is the parties. In heaven, we won't grow old, but we will have lots of parties. The biggest party will be the celebration of "the wedding feast of the Lamb," when we celebrate our new life in heaven with Jesus. It will be ten times more fun than any birthday you've ever had.

The things we enjoy here on earth are like appetizers. They give us only a taste of what heaven will be like. The things you enjoy here on earth will only be better and greater in the presence of God.

KEY VERSE: *And the angel spoke to me. He said, "Blessed are those who are invited to the wedding feast of the Lamb." (Revelation 19:9)*

RELATED VERSES: *Isaiah 25:6-8*

NOTE TO PARENTS: *Heaven lacks a lot of the things that kids enjoy—toys, television, and games. This confuses many kids because they think they need these things to be happy. They don't realize that enjoyment of kid things depends on their being kids. In heaven they won't be kids anymore—they'll be perfect, so they'll enjoy different things. What will make us happy in heaven will match who we will be then, and that's something we can't see very well right now (1 Corinthians 13:12).*

Q: WILL YOU SEE YOUR GREAT-GREAT-GRANDPARENTS IN HEAVEN?

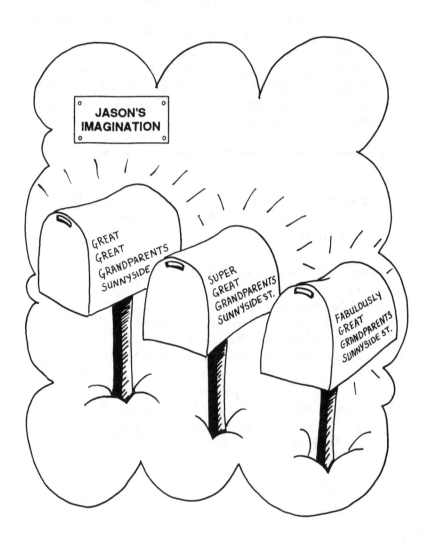

173

A: All people who have ever believed in Jesus, no matter how long ago, will be in heaven. If your great-great-grandparents believed in Jesus, they will be there. Even though you have never met your great-great-grandparents, you will be able to meet them there. But not every person who ever lived has believed, so not every person will be there.

KEY VERSE: *God has reserved for his children the priceless gift of eternal life. It is kept in Heaven for you. It is pure and spotless. It is beyond the reach of change and decay. (1 Peter 1:4)*

RELATED VERSES: *Romans 16:26; Hebrews 12:22-24; 1 Peter 1:3-5; 2 Peter 1:11; Revelation 7:9*

NOTE TO PARENTS: *This kind of question could mean, "In heaven, will we see all people who have ever lived?" The answer is, "No, only those who have trusted in Christ as Savior." Or it could mean that your child is curious about past relatives whom he or she has never met. If great-great-grandparents and others were believers, this would be a great time to tell about your family's heritage of faith.*

Q: WILL WE LOOK LIKE WE DO NOW IN HEAVEN?

HOUSE
OF
MIRRORS

174

A: No one knows *exactly* what we will look like in heaven, but the Bible makes it clear that we will have new bodies—resurrected and perfect bodies. We will be different, but we surely won't be strangers to each other. We will be able to recognize each other and enjoy each other's company, just as we do here on earth—except it will be better because we'll never fight!

KEY VERSE: *When [Christ] comes back, he will change these dying bodies of ours. He will make them into glorious bodies like his own. (Philippians 3:21)*

RELATED VERSES: *Matthew 17:1-13; Luke 16:19-31; 1 Corinthians 15:35-58*

RELATED QUESTIONS: *Do you look like yourself in heaven? When people are dead, why don't they look like themselves? What will we look like in heaven?*

Q: WHEN WE GO TO HEAVEN, WILL WE GET SNARLS IN OUR HAIR?

175

A: Nope. Heaven is a place of happiness and joy—a place of no pain. We won't have irritations and frustrations. Also, we'll have new, "glorified" bodies. Our hair won't be the kind that snarls.

KEY VERSE: *Every human being has a body just like Adam's, made of dust. But all who become Christ's will have the same kind of body as his. It is a body from Heaven. (1 Corinthians 15:48)*

RELATED VERSES: *1 Corinthians 15:35-58; Revelation 21:4*

RELATED QUESTIONS: *If you just ask for something in heaven, will it just appear before you? Will there be any schools in heaven?*

Q: WILL PEOPLE HAVE SCARS IN HEAVEN?

176

A: In heaven, everyone will have new bodies, and no one will feel any pain. There will be no physical or mental disabilities. Everybody will be able to sing, think, talk, run, and play . . . without growing tired. People may have scars, but they won't look bad.

KEY VERSE: *The bodies we have now shame us. They become sick and die. But they will be full of glory when we come back to life again. Yes, they are weak, dying bodies now. But when we live again they will be strong. (1 Corinthians 15:43)*

RELATED VERSES: *Luke 24:40; John 20:27; 1 Corinthians 15:35-53; 2 Corinthians 4:16–5:5; Revelation 21:4*

NOTE TO PARENTS: *The pattern for heaven should be our pattern, too: to affirm people as they are, not reject them for being different or "imperfect."*

Q: ARE THERE ANIMALS IN HEAVEN?

177

A:

When God creates the new heaven and the new earth, he will make all of creation new, and that includes the animal kingdom. But keep in mind that the animals won't be just like they are here on earth. They won't be dangerous. They won't attack people or be afraid of us. And all of them will get along with each other; they won't need to eat other animals. The Bible also says there will be plant life in heaven, such as trees. And perhaps best of all, no one will be allergic to any of it—dogs, cats, pollen, or anything!

KEY VERSE: *In that day the wolf and the lamb will lie down together. And the leopard and goats will be at peace. (Isaiah 11:6)*

RELATED VERSES: *Isaiah 11:6-9; 55:12-13; Romans 8:18-21; Revelation 22:2*

RELATED QUESTIONS: *If God made everything, will there be dragons in heaven? Will only dogs go to heaven? Will insects go to heaven? Will there be any lizards in heaven? Will there be any birds in the new world? Will my pet go to heaven when it dies? Will there be any feathers and ducks in heaven? Will there be any reindeers in heaven? Are there going to be any mice or frogs?*

NOTE TO PARENTS: *There is no evidence in the Bible that animals will be resurrected. So we don't really know if a child's pet will be in heaven with him or her. All we know is that we will have in heaven whatever we need to be happy.*

Q: WILL WE EAT IN HEAVEN?

178

A: We will be *able* to eat in heaven, but we won't *have* to eat to live, as we do on earth. Jesus said he would eat with his people there. But no one in heaven will ever go hungry.

KEY VERSE: *Here in Jerusalem the Lord Almighty will spread a great feast. It will be for everyone around the world. It will be a tasty feast of good food. There will be clear, well-aged wine and choice beef. (Isaiah 25:6)*

RELATED VERSE: *Matthew 26:29*

RELATED QUESTIONS: *Does heaven have hotels or inns? What do angels eat? Are angels fat? Is there junk food up in heaven? What does Jesus eat in heaven? Will there be restaurants to eat at in heaven? Are there food fights in heaven? Does heaven have sections for candy, one for cereal, etc.? Will they have Kool-Aid in heaven?*

Q: WILL WE WEAR CLOTHES IN HEAVEN?

JASON'S IMAGINATION

HEAVEN

179

A: The Bible says that people will wear clothes in heaven—dazzling white robes. But people won't wear clothes for the same reasons that they wear them here. On earth, people wear clothes to protect them from bad weather, to cover their nakedness, and to impress other people. We won't need clothes to protect us from the cold because it won't be cold. We won't need raincoats because it won't be stormy. And we won't need special designer clothes because we won't need to show off.

KEY VERSE: *I saw a great crowd, too big to count. They were from all nations and lands and languages. I saw them standing in front of the throne and before the Lamb. They were dressed in white. And they had palm branches in their hands. (Revelation 7:9)*

RELATED VERSES: *Mark 9:3; Revelation 3:18; 4:4*

RELATED QUESTIONS: *Will people be naked in heaven? Do angels have to buy things? Why are some angels naked?*

Q: DO BABIES STAY IN HEAVEN UNTIL THEY ARE BORN?

180

A: Whenever God creates a person, he creates a new soul, a new person who never existed before. Babies do not live in heaven waiting to be born here on earth. The starting place for every person is right inside the mother's womb.

KEY VERSE: *You made all the parts of my body. You put them together in my mother's womb. (Psalm 139:13)*

RELATED VERSES: *Genesis 1:27-28; 2:7; 1 Corinthians 11:8*

Q: DO PEOPLE WALK IN HEAVEN, OR DO THEY FLY TO WHERE THEY NEED TO BE?

HEAVENLY CLOUD WALKERS $5.00

Fast track to the pearly gates with cloud walkers

SNOWSHOES cloudwalkers

181

A: We don't know for sure how people get around in heaven. The Bible does say that angels fly, but it never says that people have wings or that they fly around, not even in heaven. Usually descriptions of people in heaven talk about them standing or walking.

KEY VERSE: *I saw a great crowd, too big to count. They were from all nations and lands and languages. I saw them standing in front of the throne and before the Lamb. They were dressed in white. And they had palm branches in their hands. (Revelation 7:9)*

RELATED VERSE: *Revelation 14:6*

Q: DOES JESUS COME INTO YOUR HOUSE IN HEAVEN FOR A VISIT?

182

A: Jesus always visits those who let him in. On earth, Jesus often visited his friends Mary, Martha, and Lazarus. In his early ministry, he went to a friend's wedding. And just before Jesus went to the cross, he told his disciples that he would eat and drink with them in heaven. Jesus will visit all of his friends in heaven, including you. Just think—we will finally get to see him face-to-face!

KEY VERSE: *Mark my [Jesus'] words. I will not drink wine again until I drink it with you in my Father's Kingdom. (Matthew 26:29)*

RELATED VERSES: *Mark 14:25; Luke 22:18; John 12:1-3; 14:2; 21:4-14; Revelation 3:20*

RELATED QUESTIONS: *Can you have a sleepover with God when you're in heaven? Will there be a lot of windows in our house? Will we be able to walk through walls when we're in heaven? Do they have furniture in heaven?*

NOTE TO PARENTS: *Above all else, God seeks a relationship with us. That is why he created us, that is why he sent his Son to die for us, and that is why he is preparing a place for us. Remind your child that being with us matters very much to God—now, as well as in heaven.*

Q: WHAT WOULD HAPPEN IF I ACCIDENTALLY SWORE IN HEAVEN?

183

A: You will *never* accidentally swear in heaven, because no one in heaven can sin. You cannot do wrong in God's presence. Jesus will make all of his people perfect, like himself, so you won't *want* to sin. Messing up is one thing you'll never have to worry about again.

KEY VERSE: *Yes, dear friends, we are already God's children. We can't imagine what it is going to be like later on. But we do know that when he comes we will be like him. We shall see him as he really is. (1 John 3:2)*

RELATED VERSE: *1 Corinthians 13:12*

RELATED QUESTIONS: *Is heaven as nice as we think? If I swear, will I go to hell when I die?*

NOTE TO PARENTS: *The real concern here may be that your children do not feel they are good enough to get into heaven. Assure them that if they believe in Jesus as their Savior, they will go to heaven. Also, as they pray and trust God to help them, they will become more like Jesus.*

Q: DO YOU PRAY IN HEAVEN OR JUST TALK TO GOD FACE-TO-FACE?

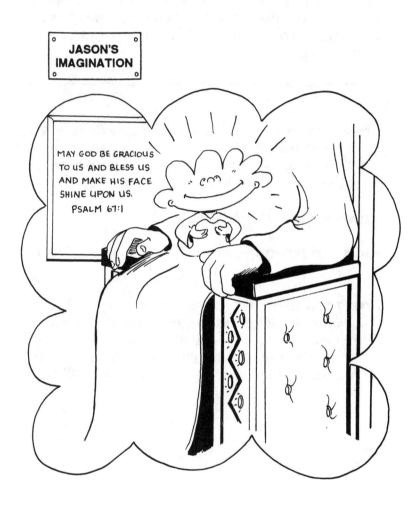

JASON'S IMAGINATION

MAY GOD BE GRACIOUS TO US AND BLESS US AND MAKE HIS FACE SHINE UPON US.

PSALM 67:1

184

A: We will be able to talk to God face-to-face. (Moses talked with God face-to-face on earth, but that was unusual.) Remember, God wants to be our friend. Right now we are separated a little, and we have to pray to talk to God. But that relationship will be made perfect in heaven. Finally we will be able to go right up to God and talk to him, just as we have always wanted to do. In heaven, we will see God just as he is.

KEY VERSE: *We can see and understand only a little about God now. It is like we were looking at his reflection in a poor mirror. Someday we are going to see him face to face. Now all that I know is hazy and blurred. But then I will see everything clearly. I will see as clearly as God sees into my heart right now. (1 Corinthians 13:12)*

RELATED VERSES: *Exodus 33:11; Acts 7:56-59; 1 Thessalonians 5:10; Revelation 4:8-11; 21:3-4*

RELATED QUESTIONS: *Will we be able to see God when we are in heaven? Will I get to see and be with Jesus in heaven? When you're visiting with Jesus in heaven, does he know what you're going to say before you say it?*

Q: WILL WE LIVE WITH ANGELS IN HEAVEN?

185

A: We will live with God and the angels. But the angels will not be equal to us there. The angels are God's messengers, his servants. Part of the angels' job is to help us here on earth. Our friends and family in heaven will be the people we have known here on earth and other Christians who have died. Remember, angels aren't people; they're God's servants.

KEY VERSE: *Don't you know that we will judge the angels in Heaven? (1 Corinthians 6:3)*

RELATED VERSES: *John 14:3; Hebrews 1:14*

RELATED QUESTION: *Who will live with angels in heaven?*

186

A: There will be no churches or temples in heaven because we won't need them. We will be right there in the presence of God. We will be perfect and sinless, so we won't need to go to Sunday school to learn about God or about how to obey him. We won't need worship leaders because we will worship just by being there. We will know God and see him face-to-face.

KEY VERSE: *No temple could be seen in the city. Why? Because the Lord God Almighty and the Lamb are worshiped in it everywhere. (Revelation 21:22)*

RELATED VERSES: *1 Corinthians 13:12; Revelation 21:1–22:17*

NOTE TO PARENTS: *After a question like this, explain the purpose of the church on earth and why it is necessary to attend. Also, if your child views church as boring, he may be asking if heaven is boring. Assure him that heaven is a wonderful, exciting place.*

Q: WILL GOD BE WITH ME ALL THE TIME IN HEAVEN?

187

A: Yes! In heaven, you will get to go right up to God and talk to him. God will be with you all the time, and you will be with him. God will be your friend, and you will be his. Getting to be with God will be one of heaven's greatest joys.

KEY VERSE: *I heard a loud shout from the throne. It was saying, "Look, the home of God is now among men. He will live with them and they will be his people. Yes, God himself will be among them." (Revelation 21:3)*

RELATED VERSES: *1 Corinthians 13:12; 2 Corinthians 5:8*

RELATED QUESTION: *Can God be my best friend?*

Q: WILL THERE BE A BIBLE "HALL OF FAME" IN HEAVEN?

188

A: Some people think that heaven is just like earth, with shopping malls, schools, athletic stadiums, and airports. But heaven is very different from earth. The focus in heaven is on God, not people. We will praise and worship God because no one's fame can compare with his.

People *will* be honored in heaven, however. The Bible says that believers will receive rewards for their good deeds. The greatest reward, of course, is just getting there. God gives salvation—a free gift made possible by Jesus' death on the cross—to all who put their faith in Christ. He will give other rewards to every believer who does good deeds for God on earth. Everyone's service will be rewarded.

KEY VERSE: *See, I am coming soon, and my reward is with me. I will repay everyone according to the deeds he has done. (Revelation 22:12)*

RELATED VERSES: *Romans 5:1; 14:12; 1 Corinthians 3:9-15; 9:16-27; 2 Corinthians 5:10; Revelation 3:5*

RELATED QUESTIONS: *Does God give out awards in heaven? Will there be a president in heaven?*

NOTE TO PARENTS: *It's easy to confuse rewards for good service with salvation by works. We receive our salvation by faith, not good deeds!*

Q: CAN WE SEE PEOPLE FROM THE BIBLE IN HEAVEN?

189

A: Everyone who has ever trusted in Christ for salvation will be in heaven, and that includes all the Bible people who ever believed. You will get to know them, too. They can be your new friends!

KEY VERSE: *God wanted them [his people in the Bible] to wait and share the better rewards that were prepared for us. (Hebrews 11:40)*

RELATED VERSES: *2 Samuel 12:22-23; Matthew 17:3; Luke 23:43; Hebrews 12:1*

NOTE TO PARENTS: *When reading Bible stories, remind your children that the stories are true and that the Bible heroes are living now with God. This should help to make the stories more real.*

Q: WHY CAN'T I SEE JESUS NOW?

190

A: Jesus went back to heaven to be with his Father, but he has *not* forgotten about his people. In fact, he is preparing a place for all who believe in him, getting it ready for when they die and go to be with him. Also, Jesus is acting as our High Priest (like in the Old Testament)—whenever his people sin, he presents his own death as a payment so God can forgive them.

You may remember that the Bible calls Satan the Accuser. That's because he tells God the believers' faults to get God to reject his people. (There's an example in Job 1:6-11.) Whenever the devil accuses a believer, Jesus defends that person. We can't see Jesus now because it's not a part of God's plan.

Meanwhile, Jesus has not left his people alone. He has sent the Holy Spirit to be with them wherever they go. That's why Jesus said, "It is best for you that I go away" (John 16:7). When Jesus comes back, he will take all believers to live with him forever. Then you *will* be able to see Jesus in person.

KEY VERSE: *It is best for you that I [Jesus] go away. For if I don't, the Comforter won't come. If I do, he will. For I will send him to you. (John 16:7)*

RELATED VERSES: *Job 1:6-11; John 14:2-20, 28; Acts 1:9-11; 1 Corinthians 13:12*

RELATED QUESTIONS: *Why did God stop sending angels to people in visions? How come God had to use angels? Why do angels come to you and not God himself?*

THE
END
OF THE
WORLD

Q: WHEN WILL THE WORLD END?

191

A: The world will not end until God is ready to take all believers home to heaven. It will happen when God decides that it is the right time. And no one knows when that time will come. Only God the Father knows. People who trust in God should not be afraid about the world coming to an end because it will be God's time of rescuing them from trouble and pain.

KEY VERSES: *Heaven and earth shall disappear. But my words stand sure forever. However, no one knows the day or hour when these things will happen. The angels in Heaven don't even know. I myself don't know. Only the Father knows. (Mark 13:31-32)*

RELATED VERSES: *Matthew 10:22; John 16:33; 2 Peter 3:10; Revelation 7:14-17*

RELATED QUESTION: *When is the world finished?*

Q: HOW WILL THE WORLD END?

192

A: The world will not end by an accident but by God's power. Right now God keeps the world safe from being destroyed. But someday, at the time he decides, God will burn up the world with fire. Then he will create a new heaven and a new earth, where all believers will live forever.

KEY VERSE: *The day of the Lord is surely coming. It will come as suddenly as a thief in the night. Then the heavens will pass away with a terrible noise. The heavenly bodies will disappear in fire [after we are gone]. The earth and everything on it will be burned up. (2 Peter 3:10)*

RELATED VERSES: *Mark 13:7; 2 Peter 3:10-14*

RELATED QUESTION: *Will God burn up the world?*

Q: IF JESUS HAS ALREADY WON, WHY IS EVERYONE STILL FIGHTING?

193

A: Jesus won over sin and death when he rose from the dead. But some people still sin and fight because they don't love or follow Jesus. Jesus is waiting for them to change their minds and follow him. As Jesus waits, they do what their sinful desires tell them to—they sin and fight. Satan has not surrendered, and he still tries to trick people. Jesus hasn't come back yet because he loves us all and wants many more people to trust in him as Savior so they can be saved from hell and go to heaven.

Jesus has won over sin and death, but he won't *make* us live at peace with each other. The more we love him, the more we learn to live at peace and not fight.

KEY VERSE: *When you understand you are useless before the Lord, he will lift you up. He will encourage and help you. (James 4:10)*

RELATED VERSES: *James 3:16; 4:1-6; 2 Peter 3:9-15*

RELATED QUESTION: *Why hasn't Jesus come back yet?*

Q: WHAT HAPPENS TO THE BAD PEOPLE WHEN JESUS COMES BACK?

194

A: When Jesus comes back to earth, people who know Jesus will be glad. But people who don't know Jesus will be very sad and afraid because they will be judged for their sin. Those who have not believed in Jesus as their Savior will be punished and sent to hell, far away from God. That is one of the reasons God urges us to tell our friends about Jesus—so they can join us and God in heaven.

KEY VERSE: *[Nonbelievers] will be punished in everlasting hell. They will be forever separated from the Lord. They will never see the glory of his power. (2 Thessalonians 1:9)*

RELATED VERSES: *1 Corinthians 4:5; 2 Thessalonians 1:6-10; 2 Timothy 4:1; Jude 1:14-15; Revelation 20:11-15*

RELATED QUESTIONS: *Will everyone see Jesus when he comes back? Does God ever fight back? Does God fight everyone that is or was bad? Will the bad people be crushed when the new Jerusalem lands on them?*

NOTE TO PARENTS: *Be careful not to divide the world between "good people" and "bad people." Many so-called good people don't trust in Christ, and they will be judged for their sin. Meanwhile, some Christians do bad things, yet they will receive eternal life because of their faith in Christ.*

Q: HOW CAN GOD MOVE A WHOLE CITY DOWN TO EARTH?

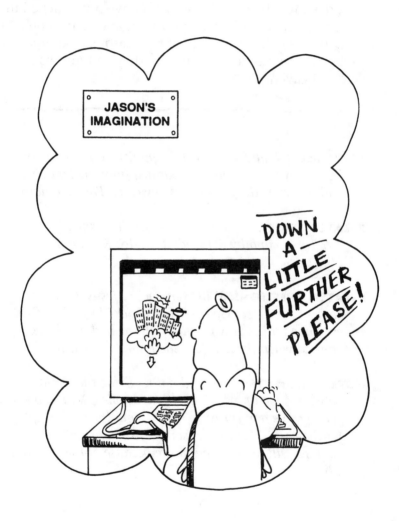

195

A: The apostle John had a vision of God bringing the new Jerusalem, the Holy City, down from heaven. We don't know exactly how this will work, but it will happen—God can do anything. He created all the stars and planets, as well as all the plants, animals, and human beings. He can certainly create a new city and bring it to earth.

KEY VERSE: *And I, John, saw the Holy City, the new Jerusalem. It was coming down from God out of Heaven. (Revelation 21:2)*

RELATED VERSE: *Revelation 3:12*

RELATED QUESTION: *What's going to happen to the houses and buildings on earth when the new Jerusalem comes?*

Q: WHEN JESUS COMES TO GET US, WHAT WILL HAPPEN TO EARTH AND EVERYONE ELSE?

196

A: When Jesus comes back to rescue all who believe in him, several things will happen: (1) Jesus will bring life on earth to an end. (2) Jesus will judge everyone. (3) Jesus will create a new heaven and new earth. (4) We will begin eternal life with God. (5) The devil, his demons, and all unbelievers will begin their eternal death in hell.

KEY VERSE: *Then I saw a new earth and a new Heaven. The first earth and Heaven had disappeared. And there was no more sea. (Revelation 21:1)*

RELATED VERSES: *1 Thessalonians 4:16-17; 2 Peter 3:10; Revelation 21:1–22:21*

RELATED QUESTIONS: *In the new Jerusalem will I be Jewish? Will God still be making things in heaven? Who's the archangel who blows the trumpet? Jesus said he wouldn't destroy the earth by rain anymore, but could he destroy it by fire?*

197

A:
No one knows when Jesus will come back, not even the angels. God has chosen not to tell us. God has also warned us not to listen to people who say they know when Jesus will return. The day of Christ's return will come "like a thief in the night," when no one is expecting it. People who say they know the date of Christ's return are just trying to trick you. You don't have to worry about missing Jesus when he returns. When Jesus comes back, it will be obvious to everyone. All people all over the world will know.

KEY VERSE: *No one knows the date and hour when the end will be. Not even the angels know this. No, not even God's Son knows this. Only the Father knows. (Matthew 24:36)*

RELATED VERSES: *Matthew 24:23-24, 36-44; Luke 21:8-9; 1 Thessalonians 5:1-11; 2 Thessalonians 2:1-6; 1 Peter 4:7*

RELATED QUESTIONS: *When will the world see God? Will Jesus be able to see everyone at once when he comes back? Does Jesus know when he's coming back? Will everyone see Jesus when he comes back? How could we see Jesus if he comes back on the other side of the earth? Will we hear something when Jesus comes back so we'll know to look up in the sky?*

MISTER
AND
MISCELLANEOUS

198

A: No. Some people in the Bible thought they saw a ghost (a spirit) at times. When the disciples saw Jesus walking on the water, they thought he was a ghost. When an angel freed Peter from prison and his friend Rhoda saw him, she thought she was seeing "his angel." When Jesus appeared to his disciples after he rose from the dead, he said he was not a ghost. And some Bible translations use the word *ghost* to mean "spirit." But the Bible does *not* teach that spirits fly around visiting people. Many people have believed that after death, people come back as ghosts. But that's not taught in the Bible at all.

Some people call the Holy Spirit the Holy Ghost. When Jesus left the earth, he sent the Holy Spirit to live within us. He is the one who comforts, guides, and protects us.

KEY VERSE: *Then the Father will send the Comforter to you. The Comforter is the Holy Spirit. He will teach you much. And he will remind you of everything I myself have told you. (John 14:26)*

RELATED VERSES: *Matthew 14:26; Luke 24:39; John 14:15-26; Acts 12:1-19*

RELATED QUESTIONS: *Did God make ghosts? Can people come back from heaven to visit earth?*

Q: WHY DO SOME PEOPLE BELIEVE IN GHOSTS?

199

A: A ghost is a disembodied spirit—the spirit of a person separated from the body. Some people believe in ghosts because they have heard about them on television shows, in movies, and in cartoons, and because many other people believe in ghosts. Some people believe in them because they have had strange experiences that they can't explain, and they figure that ghosts are the only answer.

The Bible gives no evidence that people come back to earth without their bodies. When you die, God takes your spirit from earth forever—believers into God's presence, unbelievers to a place of suffering. People do not come back as ghosts.

KEY VERSE: *It is planned that men die only once. And after that comes judgment. (Hebrews 9:27)*

RELATED VERSES: *Matthew 14:26-27; Luke 16:19-31; 24:37-39*

RELATED QUESTIONS: *When you are dead and you're up in heaven, could you talk to somebody on earth still? How can people come back from heaven when the doctors bring them back to life? If someone has a heart attack and dies and goes to heaven for a couple seconds and then comes back again, is it because the doctor saves him? Can people come back from heaven to visit earth?*

200

A: King Saul went to see a medium, or fortune-teller, because he was desperate. He did not trust in God to lead him. Saul wanted to find out things that he didn't have a right to know. In the law, God had told his people that they should never get involved with witchcraft, mediums, and fortune-tellers. Saul disobeyed God and did it anyway.

KEY VERSE: *Saul then ordered his aides to try to find a medium. He wanted to ask her what to do. (1 Samuel 28:7)*

RELATED VERSES: *Deuteronomy 18:10-11; 1 Samuel 28:3-25; Acts 16:16*

RELATED QUESTIONS: *How can people see things in crystal balls? Does celebrating Halloween make God unhappy? Is a séance when a dead person talks at their own funeral?*

NOTE TO PARENTS: *Dabbling in the occult is not a harmless pastime. Satan and demons are real beings that can influence the physical world, and occult practices only invite them to do so. Don't have Ouija boards, tarot cards, or other forms of occult fortune-telling in your home, and don't let your kids use them either. Remind your child that God loves us, has good plans for us, and has given us the Holy Spirit. He will give us wisdom if we ask him (James 1:5).*

Q: WHY DO SOME PEOPLE BELIEVE THAT TREES, PLANTS, AND ANIMALS HAVE SPIRITS?

WHOOOOOO

201

A: Some people believe that trees, plants, and animals have spirits because they are confused. Plants and animals don't have spirits, but many false religions teach that they do. Only *people* have eternal souls.

At the same time, God does want us to respect the world he created. God created all living things, including plants and animals. The Bible says that all of nature groans under the weight of our sin. And some of the psalms in the Bible say, as a figure of speech, that the trees of the fields will clap their hands in praise of God. But plants and animals don't have spirits. And even more important to remember is that we are to worship only God, not anyone or anything else.

KEY VERSE: *Praise [God] for the growing fields. For they prove his greatness. Let the trees of the forest rustle with praise. (Psalm 96:12)*

RELATED VERSES: *Exodus 20:3-5; Isaiah 1:29; 55:12; 57:5-6; Hosea 4:13*

RELATED QUESTIONS: *When my pet dies, does it go to heaven or hell? Is the New Age movement when people move to a new place? What is the New Age movement?*

202

A: Newspapers print horoscopes because many people want to read them. And people read horoscopes because they believe that major parts of life are controlled by outside forces beyond their control. They look to the horoscopes for guidance.

Believers should not look to horoscopes for guidance. Only God controls what happens, and only God knows the future. If we need advice, we should do three things: (1) read the Bible, (2) talk to wise people (Proverbs 13:20), and (3) ask God for wisdom (James 1:5). If you are worried about the future, the best thing to do is to pray and tell God about your worries, ask him to take care of you, and trust him to do it (Philippians 4:6).

KEY VERSE: *[God's people] must not be serpent charmers, mediums, or wizards. They must never call forth the spirits of the dead. (Deuteronomy 18:11)*

RELATED VERSES: *Deuteronomy 18:10-13; 2 Kings 17:16-17; Psalm 147:4; Isaiah 34:4; Philippians 4:6; James 1:5; 1 Peter 5:7*

RELATED QUESTIONS: *Why do some people try to trick other people by saying they can tell fortunes? Is ESP some kind of tax?*

NOTE TO PARENTS: *Horoscopes are closely related to occult practices. It's better to turn to God for guidance, wisdom, and assurance for the future.*

Q: WHY ARE THERE SPOOKY THINGS LIKE SKELETONS AND MONSTERS?

203

A: Some people like to be frightened by funny skeletons and make-believe monsters. And they like scaring others, especially at Halloween. But you don't have to be afraid of ghosts and goblins because they aren't real. Besides, God is with you and will take care of you. Keep trusting in him to protect you.

KEY VERSE: *Be strong! Be brave! Do not be afraid of them! For the Lord your God will be with you. He will neither fail you nor forsake you. (Deuteronomy 31:6)*

RELATED VERSES: *Matthew 28:20; Luke 12:4-5; John 16:33*

RELATED QUESTIONS: *Are there such things as haunted houses? Are ghosts real? If ghosts are real, are they the devil's demons? Why are there monsters? Why is there Halloween?*

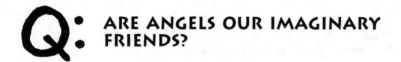

Q: ARE ANGELS OUR IMAGINARY FRIENDS?

204

A: Angels are real, not imaginary. Some people think they can talk to angels or that they have special angels who guide them. But the Bible teaches that angels are God's messengers—they serve him and do what he says. Often God tells them to help us. But they're not our friends the way people are or even the way God can be. Angels are God's servants, not people's, but they are as real as God is.

KEY VERSE: *For the Lord saves those who respect him. The Angel of the Lord guards them. (Psalm 34:7)*

RELATED VERSE: *Hebrews 1:14*

RELATED QUESTION: *Can angels tell people about Jesus?*

NOTE TO PARENTS: *A lot of children go through stages when they have imaginary friends, and many children may believe these friends are angels. This can be an ideal time to introduce them to a Friend who will always be with them—Jesus.*

Q: IF I DIE WHEN I'M A KID, WILL I MISS OUT ON DOING FUN THINGS ON EARTH?

JASON'S IMAGINATION

205

A: When people die, their life on earth ends. That's true no matter how young or old a person is when he or she dies. But do these people miss their "fun" on earth? Are they up in heaven being sad about all the fun things they didn't get to do? Not at all! Living in the presence of God is the most enjoyable thing a person can do. It is what we were created for.

Don't worry—God has a wonderful plan for your life here on earth. Enjoy the life God has given you. You won't be sorry you went to heaven when the time comes for you to go!

KEY VERSES: *Sometimes I want to live, and at other times I don't. For I long to go and be with Christ. How much happier for me than being here! But I can be of more help to you by staying! (Philippians 1:23-24)*

RELATED VERSES: *Mark 12:25; Philippians 1:21-24*

RELATED QUESTIONS: *Will there be candy and television in heaven? Do they have video games in heaven? Do I get to stay up and not go to bed in heaven? Will there be Legos in heaven? If you die when you're a kid and go to heaven, can you get married? Will there be cartoons in heaven?*